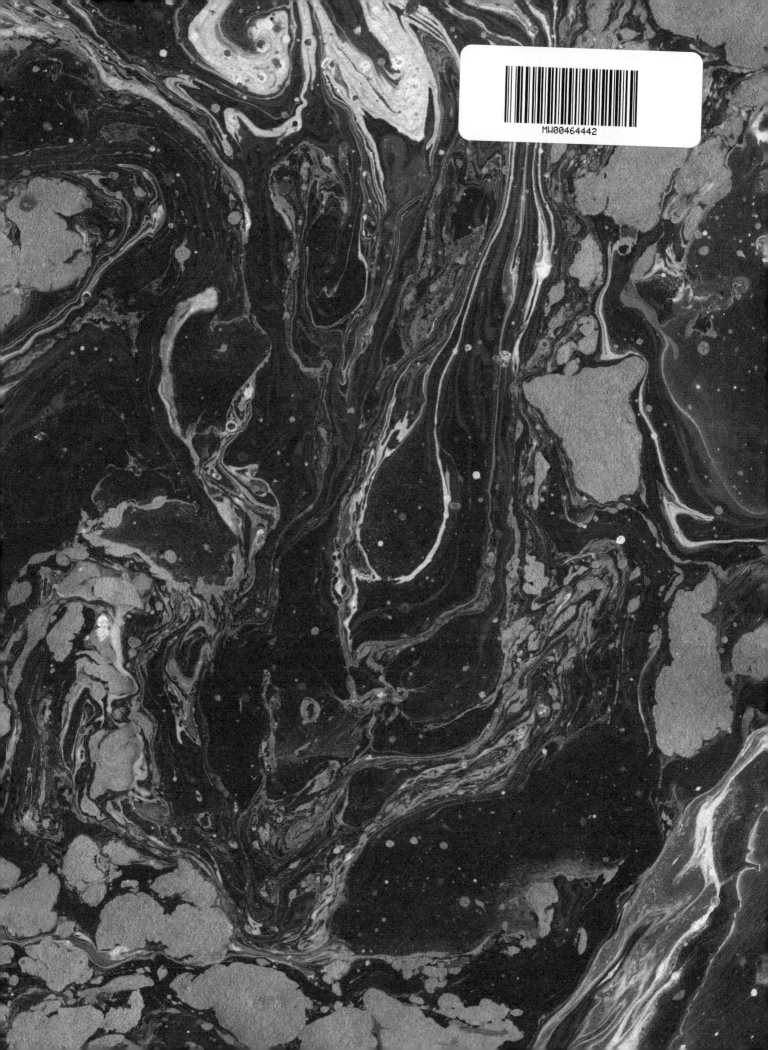

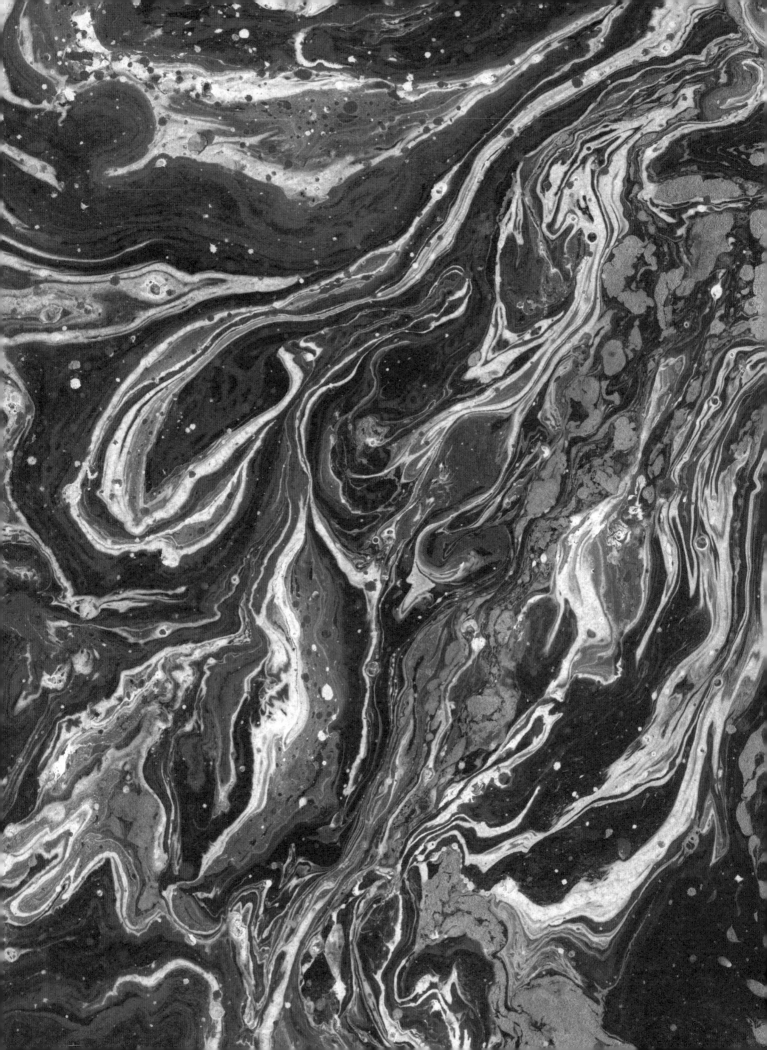

NEW ENGLAND
MODERN

NEW ENGLAND
MODERN

JACI CONRY

photography by MICHAEL J. LEE

GIBBS SMITH
TO ENRICH AND INSPIRE HUMANKIND

First Edition
24 23 22 21 20   5 4 3 2 1

Text © 2020 Jaci Conry
Photographs © 2020 Michael J. Lee

Published by
Gibbs Smith
P.O. Box 667
Layton, Utah 84041

1.800.835.4993 orders
www.gibbs-smith.com

Designed by Sheryl Dickert
Printed and bound in China

Gibbs Smith books are printed on either recycled, 100% post-consumer waste, FSC-certified papers or on paper produced from sustainable PEFC-certified forest/controlled wood source. Learn more at www.pefc.org.

Library of Congress Cataloging-in-Publication Data
Names: Conry, Jaci, author. | Lee, Michael J., 1971- photographer.
Title: New England modern / Jaci Conry, photography by Michael J. Lee.
Description: First edition. | Layton : Gibbs Smith, [2020] | Summary:
"Timeless architecture and craftsmanship fuses with modern décor to create vibrant interiors for the twenty-first century. *New England Modern* highlights interiors created by ten New England designers that are bold and vibrant, with a modern feel and flow just right for today's homeowners"-- Provided by publisher.
Identifiers: LCCN 2019028942 | ISBN 9781423653974 (hardcover) | ISBN 9781423653981 (epub)
Subjects: LCSH: Interior decoration--New England. | Architecture, Domestic--New England.
Classification: LCC NK2002 .C573 2020 | DDC 747.0974--dc23
LC record available at https://lccn.loc.gov/2019028942

FRONT COVER: Study design by Liz Caan.

BACK COVER: Kitchen design by Dee Elms.

PAGE II: Living room design by Dee Elms.

OPPOSITE: Hallway design by Jill Goldberg.

PAGE VI: Entryway design by Liz Caan.

PAGE VIII: Living room design by Tom Egan and Josh Linder.

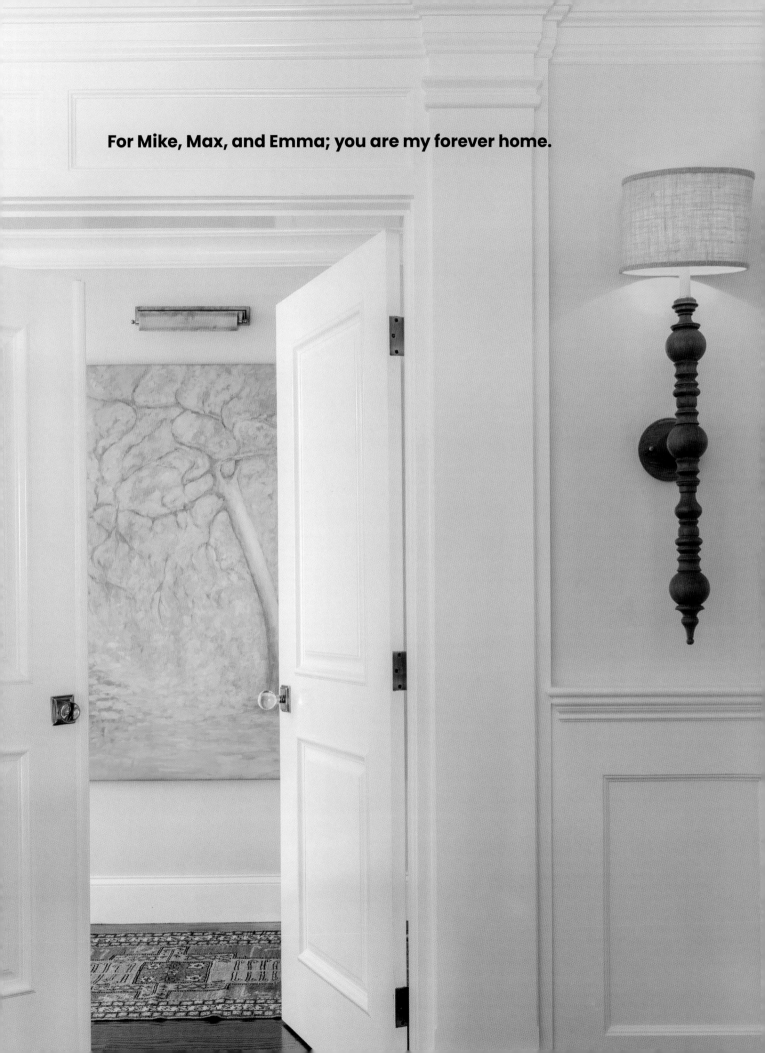

For Mike, Max, and Emma; you are my forever home.

CONTENTS

1   INTRODUCTION

9   **LIZ CAAN**
10   FINE-TUNED TUDOR
20   DAUGHTER KNOWS BEST

29   **ELIZABETH GEORGANTAS**
30   DELICATE BALANCE
38   BRAHMIN BEAUTY

49   **RACHEL REIDER**
50   SUBURBAN SOPHISTICATE
61   NATURAL SELECTION

69   **DEE ELMS**
70   COSMOPOLITAN CHIC
78   GRACEFUL REFINEMENT

87   **PAULA DAHER**
88   THE MAGIC THREE
96   PAST PRESENCE

107 **TOM EGAN AND JOSH LINDER**
108 MUTED MAGNIFICENCE
116 PALETTE PROGRESSION

127 **ROBIN GANNON**
128 MODERN REVIVAL
134 COASTAL CHIC

143 **JILL GOLDBERG**
144 UPDATED ORIGINAL
152 AIRY INFLUENCE

163 **JILL LITNER KAPLAN**
164 REFINED ECLECTICISM
172 COLOR STORY

181 **ANA DONOHUE**
182 RESIDENTIAL REBOOT
190 CLEAN LIVING

198 RESOURCES

200 ACKNOWLEDGMENTS

INTRODUCTION

I grew up in a rambling white Greek Revival home built in the 1840s. Constructed for a sea captain-turned-farmer, additions were made to the back of the house as his family expanded and the farm grew. Early on, a sprawling barn was built out back. Apple and pear trees took root in the front yard, and two horse chestnut trees were planted, which would one day reach epic heights, blossoming each May with brilliant clusters of showy white flowers.

By the time my parents bought the house in the 1980s, ill-conceived renovations and cosmetic updates that clashed with the architecture had distorted some of its original character. But my parents saw past the drop ceilings, garish kitchen finishes, and fake wood-paneled walls. They'd been entranced by the house and couldn't imagine a place with more iconic New England appeal. Clad with clapboards and topped with a red cedar shingled roof, the stately black-shuttered, seven-gabled structure stood proud. The front porch beckoned to my parents with its sky blue painted ceiling and hand-carved scrollwork; they envisioned themselves lounging there on wicker furniture, reading the Sunday newspapers, sipping coffee, and taking in the neighborhood activity.

I was five when we moved in. It took my parents nearly a decade to restore and renovate the home, a process in which every room in the house was eventually transformed. An attorney with a passion for carpentry, my father spent his weekends working on the house. He patched, plastered, and painted walls, and stripped, sanded, and stained the wide plank pine floors. He built a new hallway, removed the living room's drop ceiling to reveal hand-hewn beams, and unearthed fireplaces that had been plastered over. While professionals did the major renovations, including the kitchen's dramatic overhaul, my dad's most ambitious solo project was bringing a bedroom (which had been haphazardly transformed into a bathroom in the 1960s) back to its original incarnation. The weekend he maneuvered the old cast-iron tub down the front stairway, my mother opted to be out of town to preserve her sanity.

To be sure, fixing up that house was a labor of love. We lived constantly in a work in progress—there were months when there seemed to be a layer of dust on every single surface. But after each project's completion, the house gleamed a little brighter and my family's connection to it grew deeper.

Back then, I learned that houses have stories to tell. On our property, I found the edges and corners of the past: old coins, antique buttons, and yellowed newspapers from the early 1900s. Further evidence of the different lives led in our house came with the layers of frayed wallpaper and peeling paint, nicks in the moldings, and scratches on the leaded glass windows.

Watching my parents put their mark on our house instilled in me the notion that our homes are everything to us. Far more than just spots to converge and rooms to store our things, our homes hold our hearts. They protect and restore us.

Growing up, my dad taught me to recognize distinctive architectural details and how to spot shoddy construction. I acquired practical skills by observing him in his workshop out in the barn. As a nine-year-old, he let me strip paint off of some of those old doors, educating me about different types of wood grains. For some reason, I soaked up his home design insights far more easily than the math homework he tried to help me with at the kitchen table.

My parents had an antique trunk filled with more than a decade's worth of *House Beautiful* magazines. I'd spend afternoons flipping through the back issues, clipping pages with elements and room schemes that captivated me. I slid these aspects to be included in my dream house into clear plastic sheets, which I organized in a three-ring binder. As a teenager, I investigated my friends' houses, noting the way their parents had arranged the furniture and displayed the things that were special to them. In college, while jogging through the neighborhoods of Providence, Rhode Island, I observed houses constantly, noting their style and condition, trying to glean details about their inhabitants.

It's no surprise at all that I ended up with a journalism career centered on telling house stories. It's been a perfect marriage, this pairing of my two passions: writing and design. My work has connected me to innumerable design professionals in New England: interior designers and architects, photographers, historians, craftsmen, artists, and many other talented folks. These days, as I tour homes, learn about new design trends, and view new collections, I'm often reminded of our region's origins.

New England lays claim to boundless bits of history. Here, the past is everywhere, especially in the architecture. We are privileged to have such a storied housing stock that encompasses one of the most varied collections of residential architecture in the country. By studying the regional vernacular, it's possible to surmise how those before us lived, beginning with the austere wooden homes that the earliest colonists constructed. As that period ended and the eighteenth century began, colonial simplicity gave way to more elegant Georgians with grand staircases and foyers that stretched from the front to the back of the house. Soon came graceful, formal

LEFT: In the dining room of a South End residence, Tom Egan and Josh Linder created a focal point by installing a striking black glass wall.

Federal-style homes, and by the mid-nineteenth century, gabled Greek Revivals were an increasingly popular style among New Englanders.

During the late 1880s and early 1900s, Bostonians began to adapt the Victorian-style architecture that the British had introduced in the previous century. These were more luxuriant and detailed structures with plaster moldings and ornamental mantles. Around the same time, rambling Shingle-style residences, with wide porches and asymmetrical façades borrowed from Queen Anne–style homes, were being constructed along the New England coast. Throughout the 1900s, Colonial Revivals took inspiration from colonial architectural precedents, emulating historic design details with slightly exaggerated forms. The esteemed firm of McKim, Mead & White was particularly interested in the simplicity of colonial era offshoots and went on to design a large number of landmark Colonial Revival residences throughout New England that exhibited Georgian and Federal attributes.

Surrounded by all of this history, is it challenging to encompass a modern design perspective—to create forward-thinking interior spaces? I'm asked this often by editors in other parts of the country. For a long time, the answer to that question was yes. New England is deeply prideful of its place in history and has taken great pains to protect it. Boston was heavily involved in the early 1900s Arts and Crafts movement, a period inspired by British visionary and pattern designer William Morris, who professed that all household objects should be beautiful and useful. Yet even as Boston was championing for forward-thinking design reform and a leader in art and craftsmanship—it was home to several woodcarving studios and pottery firms that helped popularize the use of glazes and decoration—the city was nostalgic for its past. At the time, Boston's Back Bay was booming with residential construction, and houses were commissioned in revival styles, an undeniable reflection of the city's appreciation for the past. During this period, up went numerous brickclad brownstones. The brownstones were heavily influenced by Victorian architecture, as their styling favored vertical emphasis—a necessity given the tight confines of a city block. Lined with those gracious long-windowed residences and enhanced with a verdant landscape, the neighborhood obtained a symmetrical beauty that has become one of the city's enduring landmarks.

The Arts and Crafts era also influenced New England's robust furniture-making trade, an industry the region had been highly influential in since the 1700s. While furniture makers ventured into crafting more eclectic and imaginative details, most pieces were fashioned in revival styles, including Gothic and Rococo.

While other Arts and Crafts centers throughout the country adapted the Art Nouveau style—an aesthetic inspired by natural forms, particularly the curved lines of plants and flowers—Bostonians frowned upon it. The collective consensus on the style was that it exuded an excessive sensuousness that did not suit New England.

While the Boston Society of Arts and Crafts has endured since 1897, the city's enthusiasm for the movement dwindled by the 1920s. There was less value put on developing handcrafted elements for the home, and less emphasis put on exploring design concepts. "That late nineteenth– and early twentieth–century period was a time in which Boston was very aware of design," says Evolve Residential's Tom Egan. "Yet that passion for design died out here through the rest of the century. The city became stagnant; nothing was really happening here design-wise for a long time."

By the 1930s, Boston's first families furnished their homes with family heirlooms. In an effort to keep up with the esteemed Brahmins, the nouveau riche scoured local markets for antique furniture. Houses were accessorized with subdued artwork—maritime scenes, cherished family portraiture, European landscapes—that paired well with gilded finishes and dark wood detailing. Color palettes centered on brown and black, woodsy and olive greens, claret red, and, perhaps, a punch of mauve.

For the rest of the century, even as Modernism and International style influenced parts of New England, most of the region remained rooted in that restrained, predictable aesthetic.

What I tell my colleagues in response to the question about New England's current design vibe is this: while changes have been gradual, a steady inching over time, the design scene here has come full circle. Forward-thinking and multifaceted, today's interiors reflect a fusion of styles, eras, and art. There are no universal standards: unpredictable elements, contrasting materials, and juxtapositions are highly regarded. Sophistication can be combined with whimsy, rustic can coexist with streamlined, and the myriad ways that modern meets traditional are boundless. The staid sensibility is gone; New England

has shaken its stodgy reputation at last. And oh, it was worth the wait.

As the editor of a design magazine, I've had a front-row seat in this aesthetic evolution, and the privilege of working with New England's gifted interior designers. This worldly group of individuals is committed to creativity, to experimentation, and to turning tradition on its side while judiciously honoring and accentuating cherished time-honored architectural detailing.

These celebrated designers aren't solely responsible for this shift. Today's homeowners are a different breed than their parents and grandparents were. They crave more spirited rooms and are willing to take risks and embrace—though often tentatively at first—bolder aesthetics. Most of these New England homeowners savor the region's treasured architectural forms. They are drawn to homes with classic lines that may recall the forms of the houses they grew up in. Yet, as Dee Elms and several other designers featured in this book told me, "They definitely don't want the interiors of their houses to look the way their childhood homes did."

Indeed, I have to laugh at that one. As much as my parents' house means to me, as much as it shaped the paths I've taken in my life, the home I share with my husband and children is dramatically different. In elementary

school, I spent weekends in the back of my parent's Saab traveling to antique stores near and far; at night, they went to auctions where they bid on furniture they felt would have permanence in our home. On Sunday mornings, I'd wake before them, roaming the rooms of our house in search of their acquisitions. Occasionally, there would be an antique acquired especially for me: my parents once brought home a wooden cradle just the right size for my doll; another time, they had the winning bid for a miniature mahogany desk chair that swiveled like the one in my father's office.

Huge oriental rugs—that you had to be very careful of—were laid atop most of the floors in my parents' home. Dark green dominated the front hall and living room. In the dining room, there was a polished brass chandelier and an oil portrait of a serious woman from my mother's family, several generations back. Growing up, those furnishings combined imparted great comfort to me. Yet today, the ample nineteenth-century cupboard in the living room, the antique chests and the dining table—used as a counting station in a 1900s bank—simply aren't my style. My home is bright and colorful, with graphic rugs and an array of art, from vibrant paintings made by my children to delicate Asian scenes to a full-size 1925 American flag framed in reclaimed wood. This meld probably wouldn't feel right in anyone else's house, but it feels perfect for us. And that's what designer Jill Litner Kaplan asserted to me in one of our conversations. "For a long time, people wanted to furnish their homes with things that were lasting and timeless, and that's still true for the most part," she says. "Yet it has also become important to fill your home with an eclectic grouping of things that are special in and of themselves and special to you."

That's a big part of what makes this new generation of interior design so compelling. Spaces are deeply personal now, demonstrative of a feeling of unabashed freedom to pair the old with the new, and to blend items that might not be worth much, but are close to the heart.

With two elementary school–age kids and a rambunctious goldendoodle bustling around my house, nothing we have is too precious. We have large sofas perfect for flopping on and throw pillows galore, along with a farmhouse-esque dining table and shelves to display pottery my husband and I have collected during our years together. Books are stacked in several spots; I find a particular beauty in the assortment of their colored spines.

In our kitchen, we installed a sky-blue painted beadboard ceiling that recalls my parents' porch, but the rest of it is crisp white and modern, much different than the traditional, white-oak kitchen of my childhood home. Though, one of my most cherished pieces of furniture is a secretary desk my grandmother received for her wedding in 1937. In the 1960s, she painted it a dingy shade of gray, and during my childhood, it sat in a corner of her dining room. Before I put it in our home, my dad stripped off the paint and refinished the desk to its original mahogany color. The hand-carved details on the tiny interior drawers and cabinets are much more visible without the ugly paint. Every time I open the slant top, I think of my grandma writing her letters.

Each piece of furniture has a story to tell. When you create an interior with furnishings representative of multiple eras, all those stories combine to add character to your home. If a home is one-dimensional, steeped in a traditional vibe, the story falls flat. "Blending different styles from different periods in time and merging pieces from different times of your own life feels like a collection that never feels dated," says interior designer

OPPOSITE: When my kitchen was expanded, we learned that a support beam would have to run across the center of the ceiling. To turn the ugly aspect into a compelling focal point, we decided to coffer the ceiling and clad it with blue beadboard. The walls are painted Benjamin Moore Hale Navy, which keeps the room from feeling too stark white.

LEFT: The large antique flag, vivid blue drapes, and striped carpet infuse my dining room with a bit of color and varied pattern—and the elements can be swapped out pretty easily if my tastes change, which invariably happens.

Robin Gannon. "If you design a space with items spanning decades, even centuries, it becomes timeless."

The transitional furniture, the striped yellow-and-white rug, and the blue grass cloth wallpaper in my house would give my parents' historic Greek Revival an entirely different feel, and it might work. Yet if their home's detailed fireplace mantles were removed or the front porch's ornate scrollwork was replaced with a different style, then the house would lose some of its character.

And that's one of the most compelling aspects of living in and decorating a home with history, says Gannon. She recalls a client who lived in a late nineteenth-century house in Boston. "It's a beautiful, grand house. John F. Kennedy used to attend parties there back in the day. There was a lot of historic significance in the home's pedigree," she says, noting that many spectacular original details remained, including a room with astonishingly intact Zuber hand-printed wallpaper created using woodblocks, dating back to the 1800s. When her client asked if she should remove the wallpaper, Gannon urged her not to do so. "When you own an older house like that and are trying to make it more modern, you have to carefully consider the aspects you are dealing with. When taking something original out, think about how it will impact the rest of the home's history. You don't want to do something that might diminish its true nature," she says. "You can put whatever you want inside of it, but remember that you are a passerby in the life of the house; it will live long after you leave it."

Among the factors that have influenced New England's appreciation for a more open-minded approach to interior design is Boston's emergence as one of the world's top technology hubs. The booming tech sector has drawn top professionals who have lived or traveled all over the world and experienced the multifacets of design in other places, says Kaplan, who draws on her own personal experience for her work. "There's no question that my travels abroad, my time spent in France, has influenced my design sensibility," she says. "Even if your roots are in New England, this population has traveled much more than previous generations."

The exposure to different aspects of design and varied life and professional experiences has led people to become aesthetically more astute and conscientious, continues Kaplan. "As time goes on, people are realizing that New England interiors aren't relegated to having paintings of

boats hanging on a wall, painted either a yellowy gold, forest green, sky blue, or crimson. They now know we don't have to do it that way."

There are some who call New England not only a region, but also a state of mind. There's truth to that. The region's longevity has led to its predictable, familiar nature. Just look at the landscape, at all these iconic architectural specimens intact through the centuries. New England has certainly earned its reputation as being steadfast, true, and deeply loyal. With such a rich heritage, it's understandable that going in a new direction might be daunting. "It took Boston a little bit longer to catch up on what was happening in design elsewhere," says designer Elizabeth Georgantas. "Where New York, London, or Milan might always be in search of the next big thing, Boston likes what works. Here, the tendency is to have to see something in action to know that it works before there's a willingness to take it on."

Now New Englanders have seen and realized the success of melding different eras in design, says Georgantas. "They're embracing more comfortable, modern lifestyles that are less ornate, more tailored, and ultimately, more cutting edge."

Over the past few years, positive energy and fresh perspective have invigorated the interior design scene in New England, and Boston in particular. More and more, homes are bridging classic architecture with contemporary design sensibilities, combining nineteenth-century heritage with twenty-first-century verve. Art has played a big role in the transformation of the region's décor. "People's taste in art has changed. They're much more serious about it and willing to be adventurous with what they hang on their walls," says Elms. Room schemes are multidimensional, featuring much bolder colors than ever before, layers of pattern, and unexpected textural dimensions. Streamlined, antique, midcentury, transitional: it can all exist in cohesion.

Designers here have embraced this change with considerable excitement, and who could blame them? It's been a long time coming. "We're finally back to that point in the late nineteenth century when Boston was a hub of design," says Egan. "There's so much happening here now. It's pretty amazing to see the transformation."

Compiling the projects featured in this book has been an unbelievably special experience. I've had the privilege of touring countless homes here in New England, learn-

ing the processes of the region's premier interior designers. The homes featured on these pages are some of the most captivating portrayals of interior design in New England, and they represent a mere fraction of all the boundary-pushing design being done in the region. Let the spaces inspire, intrigue, and delight you. Let them alter your perception of New England design, because this concept of gloriously melded interiors is undoubtedly here to stay.

ABOVE: A bar gives the den of a suburban residence designed by Jill Goldberg a gorgeous place to congregate.

LIZ CAAN

An art major in college, Liz Caan has always gravitated toward color. "My color theory courses in college fascinated me," recalls Caan, a native of the Midwest who had a vivid imagination as a child. "It was pretty rural where we lived; I like to say I grew up in an ugly brown house." To combat boredom, Caan created things, from colorful artwork to imaginary worlds. Caan says she didn't even realize she could make a career in interior design until after college. "I started reading *Elle Décor* and *Architectural Digest* in my twenties, and I was fascinated by design and the way some designers were using color."

So Caan started experimenting. "I painted stripes and crazy colors in the apartments and houses my husband and I lived in before we had kids. We never got our security deposits back, but it was how I learned what ways using color worked and what definitely didn't," she says.

By the time she and her family landed in Boston in 2003, she was ready to pursue a career in interior design. "At the time, pretty much all I saw were beige houses; people would not think outside the box. Very few were willing to try color, unless it was those deep greens and blues that were typical of New England," recalls Caan. Fortunately, that changed with time. When Caan opened her design studio in 2011 in Newton, Massachusetts, she sheathed a prominent wall with lavender Cole & Son wallpaper and put lime-green chairs by the window. "People would come in and ask us what was going on. They were both shocked and interested by the color combination," she says.

Caan doesn't feel she gets much push back from clients on color anymore. "Color is a huge part of what I do—it's where I take my design risks. I love colors for the way they create energy, for how they affect people's mood," says Caan. "We're here for the people who want to do things a little bit differently, and now there is a lot more appreciation for that."

FINE-TUNED TUDOR

The scale of this 1920s-era Tudor was relatively small. "The ceilings were on the lower side, and there were little rounded windows and an arched front door, which are common traits of Tudor-style architecture," says Caan, who felt the home's updated scheme should honor those precious design details. As such, she couldn't make sense of an addition made to the house, resulting in spaces that were glaringly out of proportion with the rest of the architecture.

"There was this large family room with super-high ceilings—it didn't match the rest of the house," says Caan. To make the room feel more in sync with the home's true vernacular, she had the built-ins removed and replaced the heavy, elaborate fireplace mantle with a simple, curved bolection-style one. She infused the space with black, white, and green—a palette that repeats throughout the home. "The colors helped create this sense of an expressive house that feels cottagey and energetic," says Caan. To make the scale of the space feel smaller, she selected a Clarence House wallpaper featuring a tight black-and-white pattern of vases and a four-arm bronze Visual Comfort chandelier to act as a focal point, drawing the eye up.

Upstairs, the master bedroom was faced with similar circumstances. "It was just too big of a room," says Caan, whose solution was to build a floating wall behind the bed that doesn't meet the ceiling. While the four-posted bed rests against the wall on one side, Caan sheathed the other side with a marbled-stripe wall covering and designed a bank of drawers topped with a lovely wood counter that nestles snugly against the wall.

The house sits on a lovely tree-shrouded lot and Caan incorporated the setting into the décor in a myriad of ways. In the kitchen's eating area, vivid green wallpaper evokes palm leaves. "You see all this greenery outside, so the wall is really fun and gives the feeling that you are in an indoor/outdoor space," says Caan. The resin wicker dining chairs have an outdoor appeal, while the powder-coated frame brings black into the room, along with the mahogany table, which is stained hand-rubbed black.

In the living room, where the walls are painted a pleasing shade of blush pink, Caan introduced a few elements that nod to the setting, including the chair upholstery festooned with a deer motif. "It felt appropriate in this woodsy house," she says. A gallery wall was created with pieces the homeowners had in their collection, which includes a few prints with animal motifs; Caan brought in the tribal mask and rope-framed mirror.

The adjacent dining room has several pink flourishes, including a pair of vintage Joe Cariati handblown glass ball lamps. The walls, however, are painted black. "We went with black because I felt the room needed some drama," says Caan, noting the black-spiked chandelier. "But the pink keeps the space hip and kind of sweet."

In the family room of this suburban Tudor, Caan hung a black-and-white photograph of a horse. The colors mimic those in the Clarence House wall covering, while the subject, says Caan, is strong. "There's also a stable down the street, so the photo felt appropriate for the setting."

LEFT: In the master bedroom, a bed with an acrylic canopy has gleaming brass accents. A footboard sofa is upholstered in Pierre Frey fabric. **ABOVE:** Caan designed a bank of drawers topped with a wood counter for extra storage and display area.

CLOCKWISE, FROM OPPOSITE PAGE:
A bench with lively pillows sits on the second-floor landing. A bathroom features encaustic cement Moroccan tile floors. The kitchen island is topped with walnut. Just inside the front door, a window seat is perched beneath a small rounded window, surrounded by wallpaper from the Martin Group. In the lower-level guest room, the yellow powder-coated canopy bed is from Room & Board.

ABOVE: The dining room's Zebra Palm Sisal wall covering by Schumacher pairs well with the hand-rubbed black mahogany dining table and gray resin wicker chairs. **OPPOSITE:** A cocktail bench presents a perch at a striking Noir library table in the living room.

ABOVE: The gallery wall in the living room showcases eclectic pieces the homeowners have collected, along with new elements introduced by Caan. The sofa and side chairs are upholstered in velvet; the coffee table has brass legs and a high gloss-lacquered black top. **OPPOSITE:** From the front hall, there is a view of the dining room's Restoration Hardware table and tight barrel-back Mitchell Gold + Bob Williams chairs.

DAUGHTER KNOWS BEST

I t's not usually a teenager who recommends Caan's services. Yet in this case, it was a college-age daughter who followed Caan on Instagram and pointed her work out to her mother. "I guess she said, 'Mom, you should really hire this woman to transform the rec room,'" says Caan with a laugh. The parents, who wanted to give the fourth-floor rec room of their townhouse in Boston's South End a happy, colorful vibe, took their design-savvy daughter's advice and brought Caan and her team on board. Over the next few years, Caan would transform the whole nineteenth-century house with her signature pops of pattern and lively infusions of color.

In the rec room, the white trim and built-ins are accented by the bold pink ceiling. There's a lounge area with a herringbone-patterned rug in vibrant orange, purple, and lime-green hues, and upholstered furniture in an array of lively patterns. There's also a Ping-Pong table centered in the room and a jazzy dining nook with a custom-tufted banquette.

In the third-floor master bedroom, shades of green abound. "We added black and white to ground the space," says Caan, who notes that the ceiling felt huge. "It seemed unfinished—this big blank expanse." The solution was to put Cole & Son's Nuvolette patterned wall covering on the ceiling, part of the Fornasetti Panels collection. The cloud and wind motif has a dreamy quality to it. The Pierre Frey fabric on the headboard was inspired by the homeowners' affinity for celebrated designer Kit Kemp's carefree, colorful textiles. "It feels subtle and fresh because of all the colors in it," says Caan.

On the second floor, the living room features pink and purple. "It's playful, but the shades are more muted so it still feels sophisticated," says Caan, who integrated pieces from the homeowners' extensive modern art collection into the updated scheme. "Their art helped us get a sense of who they are. Seeing the art people gravitate toward eliminates some of the guesswork that goes into design," says Caan. "Based on their collection, we learned that we could push the envelope a little."

The dining table and chairs were from the family's former suburban home. Caan had the chairs reupholstered in a lively Manuel Canovas striped fabric and installed the contemporary Zettel'z 5 Chandelier by Ingo Maurer, a fixture comprised of a mobile made of scribbled paper notes. "The house blends a lot of the old with the new," says Caan. Not only are the home's doors and hardware original, the meticulously intact marble fireplaces with hand-carved mahogany mirrors above are too, making them some of the residence's cherished focal points.

The last room in the home to be completed was the first-floor bedroom of the daughter who set the whole project in motion. "She loves pink and red," says Caan, who festooned the windows with glorious linen drapes made of Pierre Frey's "Tutti Frutti"–colored Heather fabric, a pattern of abstracted shapes in a rainbow of hues. "I was so excited! Most people won't put those two colors together. We had a lot of fun with that room."

The project started on the top floor of the house, where Caan designed a bold rec room for the family.

ABOVE: In the master bedroom, the bed's custom headboard is upholstered in a colorful Pierre Frey fabric, while the drapes feature a Kit Kemp pattern in various shades of green. The Stark carpet features a floral pattern in gray and black. **OPPOSITE:** In the adjacent bathroom, the hand-blown violet-toned Murano glass ceiling fixture is a showstopper.

CLOCKWISE, FROM OPPOSITE PAGE: The dining set was an antique used in the family's former home. Caan invigorated the chairs with blue-and-red silk Manuel Canovas fabric for the backs and blue cowhide from Edelman Leather for the seats. Shades of pink, orange, and red keep the study—which has a gray herringbone Schumacher wall covering and charcoal-toned woodwork—from feeling too sedate. Chairs by the fireplace are upholstered in both a hot pink Christopher Farr fabric and a graphic print by Manuel Canovas. In the daughter's bedroom, Caan was excited to go wild with pink tones. The drapes, festooned with large pieces of fruit—a pattern by Pierre Frey in a color aptly called Tutti Frutti—pair perfectly with the more subtle white-and-pink Cloth & Paper wall covering. In the entryway, an Anglo Indian–inspired ebony cabinet atop the vintage Turkish rug is from Bunny Williams Home.

OPPOSITE: Caan swapped out the neutral upholstery on two of the homeowners' existing chairs in the living room with a lively pink-and-red textural pattern to match the new aesthetic. The linen window panels feature a linear motif in similar hues. **ABOVE:** A dark wood coffee table keeps the luxurious lavender sofa from feeling too feminine.

ELIZABETH GEORGANTAS

Elizabeth Georgantas has always had an innate sense of interior design. "When I was growing up, my grandmother's best friend was a fashion designer–turned–interior designer, and the two of them formed my love of design," says Georgantas. "Interior design was something I was raised on, almost without paying attention; it was just part of my life."

Working as an interior designer in Boston for nearly two decades, Georgantas says that it's taken the region longer than other parts of the globe to become comfortable with modern interior styling. "Boston's reputation for being fuddy-duddy is well founded. There have been lots of gilded and ornate elements for ages," she says. "That look was elegant, and it had its time and place."

Georgantas now sees great progress and forward momentum in the New England design realm. "Boston is a city that is forward thinking in many ways, and now the focus is on bringing design up to speed. With more diversity than there has ever been in the design community, there's a willingness to explore being modern in a historic atmosphere."

One of the most exhilarating parts of Georgantas' work is tackling the challenge of respecting a structure's past and making it work for the modern homeowner. "Figuring out how to make it feel young or glamorous—that's the exciting stuff: pulling it all together."

DELICATE BALANCE

The homeowners of this tucked-away Martha's Vineyard haven wanted the aesthetic to be "completely user friendly," says Georgantas. "They didn't want to worry about sand and wet bathing suits." As such, most fabrics throughout the home are indoor/outdoor, while rugs are made of unfussy and durable sisal and jute.

The couple also sought to approach the home's design with their young children in mind, focusing on fun and playfulness. Note the slide—inspired by experiential sculptor Carsten Höller and his slides at the Tate Modern—accessible from the second-floor landing that empties into the living room on the first floor. There's also a secret room beneath the stairs, inspired by Harry Potter, and in the second-floor bunkroom, a loft in the shape of a boat with a lighthouse Georgantas designed within the natural curve of the wall, replete with an actual old Fresnel lens.

The home's whimsy is balanced with cultured elements. "The couple are avid art collectors and there are several points of sophisticated interest. Every space has a story to it, and we were very deliberate about how the different spaces related to one another," says Georgantas. Curved elements, for example, are incorporated multiple times throughout the décor. In the living room, the large-scale fireplace surround is made of a curved tile that emulates the look of waves. "It was important that the fireplace not distract from the two pieces of art on each side," says Georgantas, noting a piece of scrolled metal on the wall and a tall, mirrored sculpture on the other side. "The fireplace actually became a piece of art in and of itself, so now there are three pieces of art."

The kitchen backsplash features a hand-painted mosaic Moroccan tile in another curved, wave-like motif. Above the island, a striking chandelier of different size blue-green glass vessels by WonderGlass has the unmistakable look of harbor buoys. "I saw it at Art Basel and I knew right away it would be perfect for the space," says Georgantas. A panel between the ceiling and the molding is painted a similar shade of blue green. "I wanted the ceiling to reflect color without feeling overwhelmingly blue or like a giant land of sea green," says Georgantas. The painted panel presents the perfect option for a toned-down dash of cohesive color.

The master bathroom exists in a rotunda where arches abound: both the vanity and shower are curved and the New Ravenna tile features various shaped arcs in pale pink and white tones. "The tile really reminded me of the inside of a conch shell in both color and pattern," says Georgantas. A striking antique pink-hued Murano glass chandelier draws the eye up—a show-stopping element that even rivals the room's sublime ocean view.

The ample, curved Mitchell Gold + Bob Williams sectional is oriented toward the ocean view. By the fireplace, custom chairs with slightly curved backs and flax-hued linen upholstery are modern interpretations of the classic armchair.

ABOVE: The Rug Company stair runner, in a custom shade of blue, features fish swimming upstream. **RIGHT:** A panel next to the stairway opens to reveal a secret room à la Harry Potter.

ABOVE: The kitchen's mosaic Moroccan tile features a curved motif; the ceiling is painted Benjamin Moore Windy Sky. **OPPOSITE:** The master bathroom's New Ravenna floor tile reminded Georgantas of the inside of a conch shell. She discovered the 1970s rose-toned chandelier on 1stdibs.

FROM OPPOSITE PAGE: In the bunkroom, rope details and brass ship lights contribute to the nautical nature of the space. A slide provides an alternate way of getting downstairs. The kids' guest room is furnished with red Hickory Chair poster beds paired with Cavern's "library" wallpaper. In the bathroom, Restoration Hardware porthole mirrors were selected for aesthetic and function, as they contain medicine cabinets inside.

BRAHMIN BEAUTY

Lined with gaslights, gracious Federals, and Victorian row houses built during the 1880s for the city's elite, Beacon Hill is arguably Boston's most picturesque area. Honoring the architectural origins of this brick residence in the neighborhood was crucial to Georgantas, who filled the home with many vintage elements. However, it was equally important that the home feel modern and bright.

"The whole house felt so dark. There was mahogany wood everywhere. It's located on a heavily shaded street, so there wasn't a lot of natural light coming in on the lower levels," says Georgantas. In the living room, she removed the dark woodwork and designed wall tracings for the fireplace wall. "The walls were very boring. Most of the original moldings were no longer there. The wall tracing makes the area feel more dressed up," she says. On either side of the new streamlined fireplace hang vintage tubular brass sconces by Pietro Chiesa. When Georgantas discovered there was only one sconce available, she had an exact replica made to create a pair.

Since the main entrance of the home is part of the living room, Georgantas called for the installation of a frosted-glass wall to close off the entry, creating a sense of distinction between the two spaces. She designed a sizable curved sofa that fits snugly under the windows. "It's a smaller, awkwardly-spaced room. The homeowners wanted to entertain in here. The sofa can fit a lot of bodies," says Georgantas, who also designed sleek leather "fireside chairs," which can be moved around the room.

In the dining room, the mahogany walls were invigorated with smoky lavender lacquer paint, and a faux silver Phillip Jeffries wall covering sheaths the ceiling. "The homeowner was very concerned about the room feeling dark. The mirrored wallpaper and reflective lacquer surface makes a huge impact," says Georgantas. An antique amethyst and Murano glass chandelier emanates a lovely lavender-tinted glow.

Georgantas used wallpaper in several key spots to create interest, including the walls of the stairway between the third and fourth floors, where a textural Dedar wall covering depicts star and floral motifs. While it has a muted palette, the embossed quality has movement to it, creating a multidimensional effect. The third-floor guest room features Harlequin's Sumi wallpaper, a gold large-scale brushed geometric pattern with an abstract feel. "It's all about the movement of the wall covering," says Georgantas. "With wallpaper like this you can finish a space without feeling like you have to fill every spot on the wall with art."

The second-floor library was also paneled with dark wood. "It was handsome, but the husband didn't need a big space devoted to his home office," says Georgantas. "We put his desk in the media room on the top floor and converted the library into the master bathroom." The adjacent master bedroom had minimal closets, so Georgantas created a scheme in which the original master bathroom became a connecting hallway into the new bathroom from the bedroom; the former hallway was made into an expansive closet for the wife. The bathroom is a serene white haven with built-in millwork encasing cabinetry on one wall for the husband's clothing. The original library door was kept intact. "This way, the husband can wake up, shower, get dressed in the bathroom, and be out the door in the morning without waking up the wife," says Georgantas.

LEFT: The living room has a sectional designed by Georgantas that slides neatly underneath the windows. She also designed slim leather chairs, which can be easily shifted around the room. "I wanted the sofa to take up half the room and leave the rest of the space more flexible," she says. **ABOVE:** Just inside the front door, a floating glass table serves as a display area, as well as a spot to stash essentials in a pinch.

ABOVE: In the wife's office, a green velvet sofa echoes the emerald color of the Rug Company carpet designed by Diane von Furstenberg. **OPPOSITE:** The dark paneled study was transformed into a serene, all-white master bathroom.

Georgantas designed the cerused oak kitchen cabinetry and millwork. "With all the wood in the kitchen, I was afraid the sitting area on the other side of the room wouldn't feel balanced," says Georgantas. "I thought the wall behind the sofa would feel empty and that we'd need to fill the space with art." The solution was to clad the wall with a wood-rimmed display shelf.

OPPOSITE: In the breakfast nook, the back of the banquette is upholstered in a striped Paul Smith fabric, while the seat and chairs are upholstered in a blue Pindler fabric with red piping.
ABOVE: Paul Smith's playing card wallpaper from Maharam, paired with Urban Electric sconces topped with red shades, adds whimsy to this bathroom on the home's top floor.

RACHEL REIDER

On a trip to Thailand with her mother when she was in her mid-twenties, Rachel Reider was entranced by the region's handwoven textiles. "I loved the silks and the exotic cotton fabrics," recalls Reider, who was working in advertising at the time. "My mom recommended that I take a course in interior design when we got home." After a couple of classes in the continuing education course, Reider was hooked. She quit her job, enrolled in design school, and the rest is history.

Reider has run her own Boston interior design firm since 2006. In the beginning, she says that the design schemes she was creating were considered bold and cutting edge. Looking back on her early work, however, she feels her designs then were so much more reserved than her present work. "My natural inclination is toward color, but back then I was apprehensive about using it because interior design here was ultratraditional. People were so restrained with the elements they were comfortable bringing into their homes so, as a designer, you had to tread lightly."

While it hasn't done a complete 180-degree transformation, Reider is grateful New England's design atmosphere has considerably evolved. Her clients now seek spaces that "are soft modern and transitional. People are interested in having their homes accommodate their active lives, and contemporary family living plays a big role in many projects," she says, noting that native New Englanders tend to be most comfortable with houses that feature traditional architectural styles iconic to the region. "But they aren't comfortable with an interior that has the swag and colors they grew up with."

Reider's clients tend to have clarity about the aspects they don't want incorporated into their interiors, but are less clear about what they do want. "It's an exercise in understanding how much they want to be pushed. Often, we'll start with a versatile foundation and layer in color and pattern on smaller upholstered pieces," she says. "This way, by adding and subtracting layers, a room can be completely revived."

SUBURBAN SOPHISTICATE

Moving to the suburbs from the city, the homeowners of this spacious home designed by Patrick Ahearn, an architect lauded for creating historically-motivated residences, strove to interject an urban experience into the interior. Reider was tasked with honoring the structure's timeless architectural detailing while infusing rooms with modern flair. "A young family lives here and they love color, so we wanted the house to have a youthful, informal mood while still feeling somewhat sophisticated," says Reider, who wove a palette centered on shades of blue and purple throughout the home.

The pairing of classic and modern elements is apparent in the office, where Reider painted the mahogany millwork and ceiling a vivid blue green. "The room was too dark and very traditional before," says Reider, who had a chair upholstered in a contemporary plaid featuring yellow, turquoise, and pink stripes. "We tend to think of plaids as being traditional English country style, but the bright coloring and the exaggerated scale of this pattern feels modern."

The blue and lavender tones in the dining room were pulled from the abstract painting that previously hung in the family's former home. While the wainscoting has a formal nature, the blue-metallic grass cloth wall covering is very of-the-moment. Similarly, the juxtaposition of brass and acrylic in the chandelier "makes the fixture feel very traditional-meets-modern," says Reider. The chairs look luxurious, but they are upholstered in stain-resistant fabric, a necessity given the fact that kids' pizza parties have been known to take place in the space.

There's nothing too precious in the living room either. Curved elements, including the sofa, exude a soft appeal, and the wave-form of the alpaca wall covering has beautiful, natural variation. "The room seems very colorful. Yet when you pull back the layers, you'll notice that the foundation of the space—the rug, the buffet, the wallpaper—is neutral. Color is achieved mostly through secondary pieces," says Reider.

In the kitchen, where there is abundant white woodwork, Reider called for the island base to be painted blue and had the backsplash clad with miniature navy subway tile. "It's handmade, so there is a lot of textural variation," says Reider, noting that the Urban Electric pendant lights are rimmed with a band of navy blue that matches the tile.

There's more navy blue upstairs in the master bathroom, where the vanity proudly showcases the hue. The floor is made of a graphic-patterned Kelly Wearstler–designed tile, a shape that is mimicked in the drawer hardware. "In homes like this, you're constantly thinking about how to bridge the classic lines of the architecture and the interiors without following a traditional path, while still maintaining a cohesiveness between the two," says Reider. Here, while the mirrors and sconces have softer, updated curves, their shapes are traditionally inspired.

The homeowners' collection of glass vessels by artist Elizabeth Lyons on the dining room table is an ideal accent for the scheme of the room.

OPPOSITE: The living room color palette evolved from the blue and purple tones of the painting that had hung in the family's former home. A black-and-white checkered broadloom carpet adds another layer of dimension. **ABOVE:** By the main stairway, a slim curved blue console table introduces a pop of color, while an animal hide rug and fur-topped stool add distinct textural notes.

ABOVE: Initially a three-season space, the area off the living room still exudes a porch-like appeal with its bluestone floor, wood-clad ceiling, and abundant windows. **OPPOSITE:** The kitchen island's marble counters were replaced with more durable Pietra Cardosa granite, and the base was painted a teal-toned blue.

CLOCKWISE, FROM OPPOSITE PAGE:
A painting by Michael Hoffman brings together the family room's shades of blue, red, and purple. The custom powder room vanity features blue tones from the lively fish motif wallpaper. The kitchen table has a granite top and silver-fluted base; the chairs have woven backs and durable seats upholstered in Sunbrella fabric.

CLOCKWISE, FROM OPPOSITE PAGE: In the son's bedroom, Roman shades feature a modern take on the classic gingham checkered pattern in blue and white. The starting point for the master bathroom scheme was the graphic Kelly Wearstler tile. In the nine-year-old daughter's bedroom, gray and metallic tones are complemented by blush hues. In the master bedroom, the lofty beadboard-clad ceiling accommodates a four-poster bed. The silvery shag rug feels soft underfoot.

NATURAL SELECTION

The owners of this Shingle-style home loved the classic lines of their new residence. However, there were aspects of the interior that felt too traditional for the young family. To transform some of these elements to create a décor that was serene, sophisticated, and family friendly, the homeowners brought Reider on board before they moved in. "The wife is from the West Coast and she favors a clean, more modern and organic aesthetic," says Reider. "We went with a very neutral palette throughout the house. Rather than emphasize color and pattern, we put heavy focus on textures and materials."

In the living room, Reider had the traditional-style mantle replaced with a streamlined, modern version. "We removed the travertine surround and installed white marble with lots of intriguing veining that has a much more modern feel," says Reider. "While the existing mantle was very dainty, the new one has a lot more weight."

While the upholstered furniture in the room features mostly cream tones, the fabrics are durable—a necessity in a home with three young children. Throw pillows made of silk and cut velvet are much more delicate. "I'd never use materials like that on a sofa of a family home," says Rachel. "But on throw pillows that can be easily removed, those fabrics work." The rectangular coffee table is a focal point. Made of crackled glass with a stainless steel base, "the piece has very interesting textural movement," says Reider. An upholstered bench separates the living space into two areas, the more intimate gathering space including a sofa and a grouping of four chairs around a low table. "Someone can sit on either side of the bench and be a part of either setting," says Reider.

A key component of the project was integrating the inside of the house with the outdoors. Not only do the large windows offer unfettered views of the verdant lot from the main living spaces, Reider worked closely with Winston Flowers to create a plant program for the home. "There is a lot of natural greenery incorporated into the design," she says, noting the numerous large plants potted in rough textural urns showcased on wood pedestals.

The dining area is located on the other end of the living space. The homeowners wanted a table suitable for larger dinner parties. Although architectural columns in the center of the room made accommodating a linear dining table with leaves impossible, Reider found a pedestal table that seats ten. "With the round wood top and metal base, it had the different textural components we were looking for," says Reider, who had a custom chandelier created that features blown glass lights, which relate back to the living area coffee table.

Guests first experience the house in the foyer, a space that offers clues to the textural array found throughout the interior. An accent wall features a blue-and-white wall covering by Innovations with a shell-like appeal. A mother-of-pearl mirror hangs above a table with a rustic wood top and a hammered metal base that has an onyx lamp atop. "It's a very small area that is made interesting by creating this play on materials," says Reider.

Robust plants throughout the home fill the airy spaces with verdant color and natural texture.

CLOCKWISE, FROM OPPOSITE PAGE:
In the main living area, window treatments blend with the white woodwork so as not to obstruct the view. Multiple textures combine in the front hall to add interest, including wallpaper with a shell-like texture. A settee is positioned between the living area's two seating areas to accommodate various arrangements.

ABOVE: Blown glass spheres, hung at different heights from a chrome base, offer illumination and intrigue above the dining table. **OPPOSITE:** In the adjacent space, Reider installed a similar fixture with a different grouping of glass spheres to create cohesion.

LEFT: A window seat in the daughter's bedroom is adorned with vibrant pillows, and bursts of pink are infused throughout the space to keep it feeling youthful and fun atop a neutral foundation of the walls and rug. **ABOVE:** A wall clad with black-and-gray marble in a chevron pattern adds interest to the second floor bathroom.

DEE ELMS

Dee Elms has always been drawn to a contemporary, multidimensional design aesthetic. When she embarked on her interior design career fifteen years ago, she was sought out by clients who wanted a look that "wasn't the traditional style most commonly associated with Boston," says Elms, who heads her own firm in the city's South End. "Interior design in New England has evolved," she notes. "Homeowners want their homes to exude a more curated, blended aesthetic that captures their personality. They are far more open to possibilities."

Art, says Elms, has played a prominent role in people's willingness to embrace more daring interior design schemes. "People's taste in art has broadened, and that supports more contemporary home environments," says Elms. "When contemporary furnishings and modern art are paired together, it makes a profound impact."

Beyond a passion for details and a holistic view of how design can be both functional and beautiful, Elms prides herself on being highly attuned to her clients' values and personal style, and reading between the lines. "It's critical that the client is reflected in the design; that's what makes each project unique. Your home should feel comfortable and familiar to you, yet also take your breath away."

Elms's spaces are sophisticated, elegant, and unpretentious. She credits a rigorous process that approaches each project with a mix of intuition, expertise, and a deep appreciation for craftsmanship. "There's no magic formula; it's a hundred little things that make a project successful. It starts with being attentive to the client's needs, developing the design, then sharing and building on that vision with the client," says Elms. "Our projects are not a quick sprint, but a well-planned and calculated marathon."

COSMOPOLITAN CHIC

The interior of this city residence, housed in a brownstone built at the turn of the twentieth century, was bleak at best, says Elms. "It was white on white on white. Renovated in the 1990s, there was no personality." Yet on the first walk-through, she unabashedly confirmed to her client, a recently divorced dad, that she could make the home "fantastic."

One striking element the home did have intact was the original soaring ceiling height, a feature that infuses rooms with an elegant feel. In the living room, Elms had the walls and trim painted gray lacquer, along with the built-in cabinets she designed to conceal the television above the fireplace. An expansive window seat was crafted to offer a perch to take in the bustle below on Beacon Street. "I add window seats wherever possible. It gets people into the window and really enjoying the neighborhood view," says Elms. Among the room's furnishings are a Hans Wegner Papa Bear chair and a lush fur rug; an open circular chandelier trimmed with rock crystal dangles from the ceiling. "The mix of new and midcentury items really brings the room to a whole new level."

A hand-painted black-and-white wall covering makes a profound statement in the dining room. While dark furnishings dominate, chairs upholstered in chartreuse keep the room from feeling sedate. In the adjacent kitchen, a built-in banquette nestles up to the breakfast table, a space the homeowner insisted upon. "He wanted a casual dining space where he could eat pancakes with his kids in the morning," says Elms. "The kitchen is small, and we really didn't have room for it." Yet the designer was able to work her magic: by reducing the size of the island, there was just enough space to fit the table.

In the master bedroom, shades of gray exude masculine appeal. Layers of strong textural notes—the silk wall covering, cashmere drapes, a black-velvet headboard, and lighting made of chain mail strung from the ceiling—combine to create a distinctly modern atmosphere.

"It was such a traditional place before," says Elms. "We kept the basic form the same. Just by changing the colors and finishes, hardware, and other small things, we created this dramatically different contemporary home."

Just inside the entry, a cantilevered shelf is affixed to the wall below an encaustic work by Martin Kline.

ABOVE: Elms transformed an out-of-place wet bar into a striking focal point. **RIGHT:** Elms replaced the living room fireplace with a sleeker model trimmed with brass rivets. Storage is concealed behind built-ins painted a glossy gray lacquer, and a fur rug adds a distinct textural note.

OPPOSITE: Elms livened up the existing black kitchen cabinetry with metallic grass cloth on the walls. **ABOVE:** By reducing the size of the original island, there was enough space to accommodate a narrow banquette that slides up to a small pedestal table.

CLOCKWISE, FROM OPPOSITE PAGE: A built-in desk with shelving above makes for an attractive and functional home office enclave. In the powder room, the walls are Venetian plaster, and the custom sink is made of marble with etchings that reminded Elms of a Missoni fabric. In the daughter's bedroom—"a tiny jewel box of a space," says Elms—the wall behind the bed is sheathed with an iris emblazoned wallpaper that has a Monet-esque appeal. In the master bedroom, the cashmere drapes, silk wall covering, and velvet headboard combine to create a luxurious feel.

GRACEFUL REFINEMENT

Located in a gracious nineteenth-century building, this newly renovated, three-bedroom Back Bay penthouse had the ample square footage the homeowners sought, but the developers, says Elms, hadn't put much thought into space planning. Among the design challenges Elms tackled was creating distinction in the sizable living room. To break up the vast space, she applied molding to the ceiling and defined two separate seating areas, each one with an eye-catching Lindsey Adelman light fixture affixed to the ceiling directly above. "A custom *tête-à-tête* is situated in the middle that you can sit on to face either side of the room," says Elms.

The large stairway dominates one end of the room. Initially painted white, it stuck out in an unattractive way. "The stairs are a huge part of the living room; when they were painted white, it just felt so manufactured," recalls Elms. "Newer projects can sometimes lack soul." To turn the stairway into a compelling focal point, she convinced the homeowners that painting it black would add depth to the space, and indeed, the stairway is now an alluring architectural detail.

In the kitchen eating area, Elms created a curved banquette that follows the contour of the bowed windows. A sculptural Apparatus fixture above the table was selected for its light, airy appeal. "We didn't want to emphasize the lighting too much in here," says Elms, noting the pared down crystal glass pendants above the island. Blue accents and the glass-mosaic tile backsplash with a metallic backing invigorate the white kitchen.

Silvery blue-toned grass cloth on the walls gives the master bedroom a cocoon-like feel. Elms found the vintage blue velvet chairs at the Paris Flea Market. "The huge brass feet really makes the chairs special," she says. Aged-brass drawer pulls on the walnut nightstands infuse more richness to the room, and brass is also featured in the master bathroom, where an eye-catching geometric chandelier is made of the bright gold metal.

OPPOSITE: In the family room, a plush navy blue sectional is perfect for lounging. **ABOVE:** Elms called for the large stairway to be painted black, which dramatically enhanced its appeal.

ABOVE: Geometric ceiling molding and two striking glass Lindsey Adelman light fixtures help create definition in the expansive living room. **OPPOSITE:** Shades of gray, black, and white are found throughout the home; a Timorous Beasties wall covering in the foyer presents a particularly compelling mixture of the hues.

ABOVE: The kitchen backsplash, laid in a chevron pattern trimmed with gold leaf, breaks up the expanse of white cabinetry along the back wall. **OPPOSITE:** The built-in banquette in the kitchen accommodates the whole family for meals.

CLOCKWISE, FROM THIS PAGE: Silvery shades of gray and blue evoke a sumptuous vibe in the master bedroom. As the vanity counter is made of thick marble, the backsplash consists solely of a slim band of brass. In the master bathroom, pale pink drapes frame the tub-side window. One bedroom features an upholstered headboard that stretches to the ceiling and an extra wide window seat.

PAULA DAHER

In the early 1990s, when Paula Daher launched her eponymous interior design firm, New Englanders were focused on furnishing their homes with brown mahogany furniture. "Everything was very traditional," recalls Boston-based Daher. "A client might consider 'spicing it up' with gorgeous silk curtains and throw pillows with a little bit of color, but no one was willing to go further than that to really move outside of their comfort zone."

"People loved sets—everything in a room matched," continues the intrepid designer, whose refined approach to design is heavily influenced by her international travels; she finds Paris in particular to be a great source of inspiration. "It truly is the epicenter of style, old and new."

As interior design has become increasingly exposed through television, magazines, and social media, Daher's clients have become more open to design ideas from different periods of time. "They're more agreeable now to meld antiques with contemporary art, to mix materials," says Daher. "Everything no longer has to be so matchy-matchy."

One of the most positive aspects of this shift in perception, says Daher, is that her clients require less of an education process. "Before, if something out of the box was suggested, a client would often react by saying 'Oh! I couldn't possibly put that in my dining room!' Now, they are much more receptive to different ideas. A common reaction now is, 'OK, why do you think we should go this route?'" And most often, they'll trust Daher's creative instincts.

THE MAGIC THREE

On her initial walk-through of this 1918 English Tudor–style home, Daher encountered a choppy layout that was "not at all appropriate for the way the young family moving in lived," she says. Although the aesthetic was hopelessly out of date, the house possessed rich, authentic character.

A top-to-bottom overhaul was required before the homeowners took up residence. Daher combined several small rooms to accommodate a modern kitchen, highlighted by glorious greenish-gray quartzite counters with an integrated casual dining area and family room. While the infusion of modern elements was essential, Daher felt it was equally crucial to maintain three iconic original elements of the house.

"If these three things were removed, the specialness of the home would not be there," says Daher. The first element was the terra-cotta floor in the foyer and original living room. Although the homeowner wasn't initially sure she like the floor's strong orange tone, Daher convinced her that the hexagon-patterned tile was to be revered. The layout was reversed so the living room became the new dining room, where the floor seemed more appropriate, and vice versa. Daher designed ceiling molding laid in a hexagonal pattern that echoes the floor detailing to add visual interest to the large room.

The second aspect the designer considered integral to retaining the home's nature was the detailed mahogany-paneled walls in the library. "The dark wood felt gloomy and dated. It wasn't happy. It didn't suit the new ambience of the house," says Daher. To preserve the character of the paneling while giving it a fresh appeal, she had it stripped and restained in a light washed oak. "Now the gorgeous original green marble fireplace surround, which had barely been noticeable before, really stands out, and the room feels bright, airy, and modern," says Daher.

Finally, Daher saved the narrow mahogany railing with iron spindles on the stairway. "At first, the homeowner thought it was fussy because it's so different from the thick wood railings common today," says Daher. The railing became a compelling focal point by adding blue grass cloth to the stair hall walls, along with a modern rectangular light fixture strung from an iron chain and a woodcut print painted black. "It all works together in a beautiful, elegant way," says Daher.

In the foyer, the original front door and terra-cotta floors remain intact to honor the home's origins. Paired with a demilune table and an antique mirror, the elements set the tone for the house.

LEFT: The library's mahogany woodwork was re-stained in a washed oak, which considerably lightened the space up. **ABOVE:** A blackened steel cabinet by John Pomp, with doors made from glass rondelles set within brass circles, is used as a dry bar. The painting above is by Michael Zigmond.

CLOCKWISE, FROM OPPOSITE PAGE: The family room features a shiplap-clad wall with carved-in seating nooks and shelving. Retaining the wrought iron railing in the stairway ensured that it remained one of the home's focal points. The gray-green hued stone used for the backsplash and kitchen counter was the starting point for the room's scheme. Reclaimed wood was used for the range hook and ceiling beams.

CLOCKWISE, FROM OPPOSITE PAGE: To create a large master suite with his-and-her bathrooms and sizable closets, the home's second staircase was removed. The bedroom aesthetic is simple, with a custom bed and a few subtle glam elements, says Daher. Creating a mudroom was an essential part of the renovation. Daher designed built-ins and a window seat upholstered in apple green, the wife's favorite color.

PAST PRESENCE

A rooming house for many years, this late-nineteenth century Back Bay brownstone had been damaged in a fire. It was in the process of being developed into two residential units when the new homeowners purchased the property. The homeowners wanted the multilevel building to be a single residence, so Daher worked closely with the architect to reconfigure the floor plan. "The entire structure was a shell when we came on board; floors had been ripped out and four brick walls were in virtually every room. Very few of the original architectural details remained except for the front door, newel post, and stairway accessing all four floors," says Daher.

Daher designed moldings and trim work that pays homage to the stately structure's origins. In the library, lighter wood paneling evokes an enveloping club-like feel and a medallion inset in the cove ceiling hearkens back to the building's Gilded Age origins, while modern art and upholstery ensconce the home in the present day.

Daher typically keeps wall colors neutral to serve as backdrops for punctuations of color with art and accessories. In the dining room, a striking landscape painting takes center stage while subtle graphic patterns in neutral tones—a Steven King rug and the Dedar upholstery on the host chairs—infuse additional dimension. Since space is at a premium in the adjacent living room, furnishings were selected for their sleek profiling. "In most of the Back Bay homes we work in, rooms are long but narrow, so it's a challenge to create floor plans with furniture layouts that accommodate many people while allowing them to walk freely around the space," says Daher, noting the armless, low-profile Douglas Jennings chairs.

The kitchen accents take cues from the French blue La Cornue range and regal brass-trimmed hood above. The island is topped with soapstone with a corrugated edge that lends an informal feel to the area. "The edge adds a bit of antiquity and casualness to the space," says Daher. "The family has four boys, so we didn't want every room to feel so uptown." While the pendants above exude elegance, the glass has a lavender tint that adds a touch of whimsy.

A fifth floor was added to the top of the house to accommodate a hangout space for the boys where French doors lead to a deck that boasts a hot tub against the city backdrop. The third floor is a parents-only zone, however, as the master suite takes up the whole level. The bedroom is serene and luxurious, while the bathroom, with recessed walls made of marble, is an absolutely unrivaled space. "The walls are traditional in nature, in keeping with the architecture of the home, yet clad with stone, they feel updated and modern," says Daher. "The room is definitely a showstopper."

Among the few elements that remain original to the late-nineteenth century residence is the stair railing that runs from the foyer to the fifth floor.

ABOVE: Made of rock crystal, the dining room chandelier is striking without dominating the space. **RIGHT:** Shades of blue unify the kitchen and family room.

CLOCKWISE, FROM THIS PAGE: The home's fifth floor, which opens to a spacious roof deck with a hot tub, was made into a rec room for the family's four sons. A skylight filters light from the top floor down through all the other floors. The powder room sink is made of gray smoke onyx.

OPPOSITE: The library is small in scale and has a club-like vibe. "The intent was to make it a more formal entertaining space," says Daher. **ABOVE:** A mirror and commode by Dennis & Leen nestles neatly into a nook next to the living room fireplace.

OPPOSITE: In the master bedroom, a Tibetan wool rug contributes to a serene feel, along with the subtle wall covering that evokes the appeal of Venetian plaster.
ABOVE: The walls of the master bathroom are clad with marble.

TOM EGAN AND JOSH LINDER

After working together at another firm for ten years, Josh Linder and Tom Egan, along with Rebecca Abrams, launched Evolve Residential in Boston's South End more than a decade ago. The name of the firm can serve as an indicator of the partners' passion for the continued development of design—the urge to propel forward and push boundaries.

Over the course of their lengthy careers, Linder, an interior designer, and Egan, an architect, have witnessed an evolution within the local design scene. "For decades and decades, there really wasn't any moving forward in Boston from a design perspective," says Egan.

In recent years, however, the internet and social media have dramatically impacted the speed with which design ideas travel. "It used to be that once a project was completed, it could take up to two years for it to be published in print, and that was the sole outlet," says Linder. "Now, people are seeing projects immediately after they're photographed on social media." With all the up-to-the-minute design influences so prevalent, New England has gradually evolved to adapt a more modern design mindset.

At the center of Evolve's ethos is the fusion of art and architecture, says Linder. "We love to be informed by the history of the spaces we're designing."

Much of the firm's work is done in homes more than one hundred years old. For such projects, a classical base is the foundation that the duo loves to infuse with "new" elements: saturated colors, edgier accents, and fixtures made with innovative materials.

"Furniture layout is first," says Egan. We draw out as many room layouts as possible, carefully tracking the shape of the space and the shape of the furniture. Once we establish the layout, clients can visualize the room and the rest comes more naturally."

MUTED MAGNIFICENCE

While Egan and Linder are adept at creating interior schemes featuring bold infusions of color, they do love a challenge. For this home in an 1872 brownstone in Back Bay, the duo was asked to work with a much more muted color scheme. "We don't get a lot of projects that ask for a restrained palette," says Linder. "But we were excited to do that for this home, because it's something different for us and took us a little bit outside of our comfort zone." A calming neutral palette with hints of blue—and, occasionally, red—weaves through the rooms throughout the two-level home.

The living and dining area encompasses the front of the home's main level, where ceilings stretch to just under twelve feet high. To accentuate the room's great scale, two striking gold-plated chandeliers designed by Valentina Fontana are hung from the ceiling. "They really add a grand element to the space," says Linder. "In a historic context, back when the home was built, it's very possible that two chandeliers would have been hung in this room." The fireplace's marble mantle is original to the home; the chests on either side of the fireplace are from the 1940s, and atop, antique Murano glass lamps pick up hints of the fireplace's marble tone.

The homeowners, empty nesters, are from Italy, and throughout the space Egan and Linder incorporated Italian works of art, some of which have belonged to the family for decades. "We like to find ways to personalize the home as much as possible for the owners," says Linder, noting that he and Egan sought out furniture and upholstery from Italian lines for the interiors.

The living area encompasses multiple scenarios. At the oval Saarinen table, a curved Poliform sofa nestles around the bow of the elongated window. Not only does it serve as the home's more formal dining area, the wife often sets up her laptop on the table to work during the day. "It's a really nice spot to sit and look out at the neighborhood," says Egan. There's a more casual eating area in the adjacent kitchen, where two voluminous red Iacoli & McAllister light fixtures—each one comprised of seven open frame-like clusters—hang above the island. "Since the kitchen is mostly white, we wanted to add a wow moment. We thought these were a great way to use the space and put a little bit of our spirit in the room," says Linder.

There's another wow-worthy fixture in the master bedroom: a large-scale tiered resin chandelier hangs from the ceiling. Made from a 3-D printer, the piece is elegant with a touch of whimsy. The scalloped form of the chandelier is evoked in several spots in the room: in the nail head arcs of the upholstered headboard, in the shape of the large ottoman at the foot of the bed, and in the form of the sofa nestled in the arc of the bowed window. "We really enjoy creating playful sculptural moments like these," says Linder. "At first the eye might overlook them, but if you're really studying the space, you'll notice them right away."

In the master bedroom, a curved sofa conforms to the arch of the long, graceful windows.

The living area accommodates multiple purposes with its flexible seating arrangements, and there is much for the eye to enjoy. The dining table is nestled in the bay window, and the carved fireplace mantle hearkens back centuries.

OPPOSITE: In the kitchen, red sculptural pendants provide a pop of color and texture against the neutral cabinetry. **ABOVE:** A custom one-arm sofa serves as comfortable seating at the kitchen table.

CLOCKWISE, FROM OPPOSITE PAGE: The Phillip Jeffries Marbleous wall covering gives the powder room plenty of wow factor. On a bedroom wall, framed pages from Italian books tie into the homeowners' heritage. Upstairs, the master bedroom chandelier, crafted with assistance from a 3-D printer, adds a modern twist to the historic residence. A casual seating area is nestled between the bedrooms on the lower level.

PALETTE PROGRESSION

The first time Egan and Linder visited this five-story city residence, they were a bit taken aback. They'd come to know one of the homeowners well. "He's a very fashion-forward, edgy guy," says Linder. At the time, the 1840s townhouse the homeowner shares with his partner had a mostly beige interior that felt rather boring. "It didn't reflect any of his cool sensibilities," recalls Linder.

At the time, the homeowners were working with an interior designer who didn't have a handle on their style. Linder and Egan, however, "could translate what we saw when we looked at this cool, fashionable couple and turn it into an aesthetic for their home," says Linder, who, along with Egan, overhauled the staid décor "drop by drop," initially bringing in colorful elements one at a time. In the living room, they added a diamond-tufted green velvet sofa, an orange pouf, and red embroidered Pierre Frey pillows. "Once they realized how electric the home could be with color, they were all in," says Linder. Next came drapes in a Nicolette Mayer fabric that combines the colors in the room and introduces a hint of purple. When Egan sent the homeowner off to find two large colorful pieces of art to anchor the space, he came back with massive canvases by Jarrad Tacon-Heaslip depicting a rainbow of hues for each end of the room. "They were absolutely perfect," says Egan.

In the master bedroom, where the walls were already painted a bolder shade of blue, the designers added a multihued grass cloth to the ceiling. "We looked at it as the room's fifth surface and utilized it as an opportunity to add warmth and color," says Linder.

The sunroom, located on the top floor of the home with access to the roof deck, is dubbed "the green room." The goal was to pack the room with as many plants as possible. A verdant green velvet sectional has seats and cushions made of outdoor fabric and the multitonal green shag rug evokes the appeal of grass. Another nod to nature is a collection of paintings of bees by artist Ryan Chadwick, which is hung against an abstracted wall covering by Jill Malek that the designers selected for the way it captures the frenetic energy bees might make buzzing around the space.

In the dining room, located on the ground floor, an oversize barn door was removed to accommodate a mirrored black glass wall that adds serious dramatic appeal. "It was a very drab space. The mirrored wall adds interest and formality. It gives the room a bit of a nighttime noir, glamorous feel," says Egan. The lively green Moooi dining chairs, however, ensure that the room exudes a bright, slightly irreverent vibe in cohesion with the rest of the home.

In the office, two walls of built-ins offer abundant storage in an eye-catching manner.

OPPOSITE: The large colorful canvases that flank each side of the living room are by Jarrad Tacon-Heaslip.
ABOVE: To add more storage, the window seats were designed to have touch drawer storage underneath.

Moooi Monster Chairs in a bold shade of green provide a surprising accent within the room's black elements.

ABOVE: In the sunroom, the "X" painting is by Matt Schwenk. **RIGHT:** The lush velvet sofa has cushions upholstered in outdoor fabric for the material's "dog-friendly nature," says Linder.

ABOVE: In the phone booth–sized powder room, the brass mirror reflects the high gloss green lacquer on the opposite wall. **OPPOSITE:** The master bedroom features a ceiling clad with Nicolette Mayer grass cloth, green velvet poufs, and nightstands designed by Linder with red painted interiors.

ROBIN GANNON

When Robin Gannon first started out as a designer, she felt that most interior schemes she encountered in New England were one-dimensional. "A house would veer toward one aesthetic—a Georgian period or one or another kind of revival," she recalls. By some standards, Gannon's tenure in the industry is short. She's been a practicing designer for ten years—prior to that, she was city prosecutor and, later, a criminal defense attorney; quite a contrast from her current profession. Over the course of the past decade, Gannon has seen quite a progression in her clients' tastes.

"Now, as our information exposure has become so global, interior design has followed suit. People are no longer simply influenced by what they are seeing in their neighbor's house, but by what the design scene is like all over the country, overseas, everywhere," she says. "People want to incorporate details into their homes they'd never considered before, things they had no idea could be done."

New England's assortment of historic architecture is to be revered, says Gannon, whose studio is based in Lexington, Massachusetts, where she also operates a home accessories boutique. "There is still great respect for tradition here. But our feet are no longer in the cement. It's great to have some period pieces if you live in an antique house, but camelback sofas don't have to be everywhere." In the rooms she designs, Gannon likes to "turn the idea of tradition on its head" by blending different style furnishings from a multitude of eras. "When you do that, the décor never feels dated."

MODERN REVIVAL

With its gracious shingled façade, this 1920s Georgian Colonial had plenty of curb appeal. Inside, however, was a different story. When Gannon was hired to revamp the interiors, much of the home's original details had been stripped away during ill-conceived renovations. Updates were essential, yet honoring the original architecture was paramount. "It was important to make sure the house looked true to its origins," says Gannon, who added architectural elements back in where they belonged.

In the library, Gannon called for the removal of an over-scale Victorian-style oak fireplace surround and designed a more refined paneled one, along with matching built-in cabinetry with mirrored fronts, all painted a warm light gray. "The goal was to make the room feel like a library, without the stuffiness of a library," says Gannon. Rather than fill the room with bookcases, an airy atmosphere was established with the addition of a slim bookshelf above the drapery rods that rim the room.

In the family room, moldings and paneling were added and painted the same white as the walls. Creating a calm backdrop was necessary, as the space showcases several pieces of contemporary art. "One of the ways you can bring different time periods together is through art," says Gannon. Transitional furniture, including a pair of clean slope arm chairs and a track arm sofa, exists in harmony with a modern Lucite chair. "You can have more freedom with furniture and artwork. But when blending the old and new, I tend to keep the things that get attached to houses, such as lighting, more consistent with the architecture of the structure," says Gannon, citing a French antique–style sconce made of gilt iron and crystal by Niermann Weeks that she selected for the library.

Pops of color are infused in the artwork and other surprising spots; the inside of the dining room chairs are upholstered in a cheerful yellow leather. While the structure of the chairs is more traditionally styled, the chunky blue-lacquer table has a decidedly contemporary form. "The table is so unexpected that it acts as a piece of art," says Gannon.

Painted a rich gray with white trim, the molding honors the home's origins, while strategic elements, like the vintage framed advertisement turned on its side, have modern appeal.

ABOVE: On one end of the library, a low-backed sofa offers a pleasing place to stretch out and enjoy the view. **OPPOSITE:** At the other end of the room, a handsome desk is paired with Lucite chairs with faux zebra-hide seats.

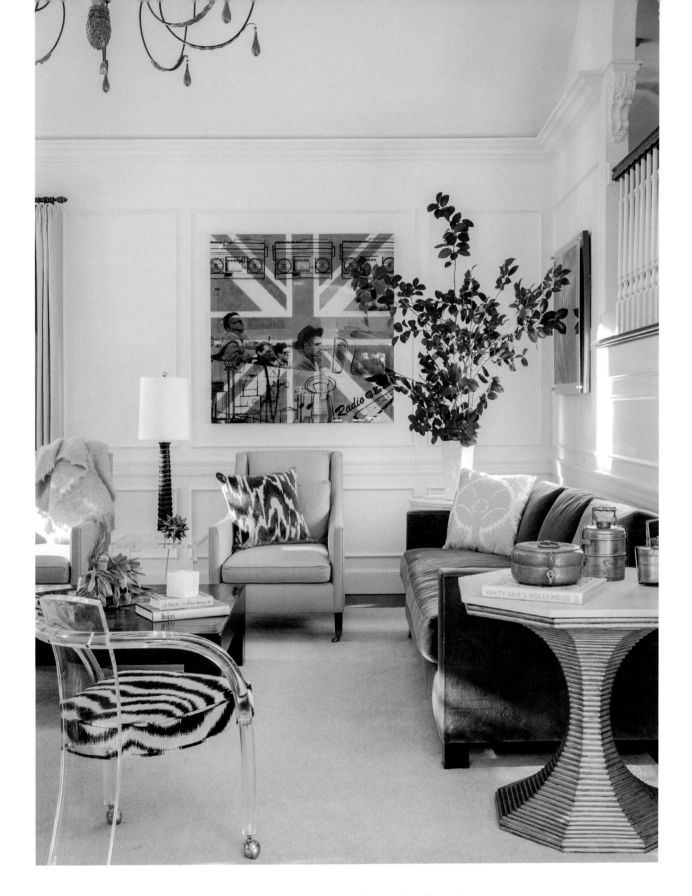

OPPOSITE: Classic leather club chairs are jazzed up with ikat print pillows in a rainbow of hues. **ABOVE:** The white living room walls act as a great backdrop for pieces from the homeowner's collection of contemporary art.

COASTAL CHIC

This airy, secluded retreat is oriented toward a bucolic harbor on Cape Cod. The homeowner was geared up to embrace a color-saturated décor, which delighted Gannon. However, the designer proceeded with caution. "In waterfront homes, you have to use color with a bit of restraint. First and foremost, the aesthetic has to be about the location and the view," she says. "If you fill the space with too many patterns and colors, your eye doesn't know where to go. If there is too much contrast, the space can become too energetic." White-painted walls and woodwork created a calm shell for infusions of blue and yellow throughout, along with "the quintessential colors of New England," says Gannon: hints of red, white, and blue.

In the vast open room containing the kitchen, living, and dining areas, the separate spaces are delineated with tray ceilings, strategic furniture placement, and statement-making light fixtures. Rectangular blue-trimmed pendants hang above the dining tables. "I love these pendants, because they have a little color on the inside but are also glass, so you can see through them toward the view," says Gannon. She also encouraged the homeowners, empty nesters, to put two smaller dining tables in the room that can be pushed together, rather than one large one. "While the couple's adult children often visit, a lot of the time it's just the two of them at the house. I didn't want them to feel lonely on those occasions sitting at this big table for ten people."

In houses near the water, it's essential that materials be impervious wherever possible. Sisal rugs throughout mask sand, while indoor/outdoor fabrics were used as upholstery. "Every piece of furniture needs to be able to sustain wet bathing suit bottoms," says Gannon. "It's very relaxing to know that you don't have to worry about bringing sand into the house or anything precious being ruined."

In the master bedroom, the blue grass cloth on the walls is a departure from the white walls in most of the home's other rooms. A rough sewn sliding barn-style door with a stainless steel European-style pull separates the bathroom. "It presents an interesting juxtaposition of rustic and traditional meets modern," says Gannon. A mirror over the dresser is patterned in a fish scale motif and the woven light fixture hanging from the ceiling has restrained beach flair. In the adjacent master bathroom, the entire wall behind the sink is sheathed with glass tile that has the distinctive appeal of sea glass. "While one might not know the location of the house, all the subtle elements add up, and if you look at them carefully, you'll figure out the type of setting it is pretty quickly," says Gannon.

OPPOSITE: An expansive wall across the back of the open kitchen, living, and dining areas makes the serene vista feel like part of the room. **ABOVE:** Sisal and other natural fiber rugs were used in all of the bedrooms.

ABOVE: In the sunroom, Janus et Cie white woven chairs and neutral sofas are paired with tables that evoke oversize river stones. "They are great focal points," says Gannon. **OPPOSITE:** The whimsical painting of the synchronized swimmers is from Jules Place, an art gallery in Boston's South End.

ABOVE: Neutral-toned cabinetry almost recedes into the molding; it was essential that none of the kitchen's functional elements interfered with the view. **OPPOSITE:** In the dining area, the yellow cabinet was once gray. "It was painted and then over-glazed so you can still see the grain of the wood," says Gannon.

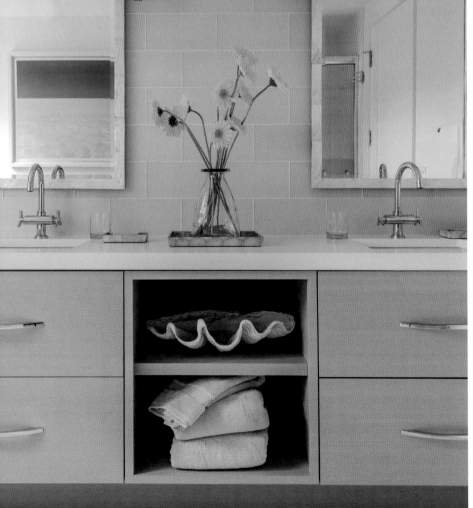

CLOCKWISE, FROM OPPOSITE PAGE: A sliding barn door separates the master bedroom and bathroom. Vibrant plays on turquoise and yellow enliven a twin bedroom. The green glass tile in the master bathroom recalls sea glass.

JILL GOLDBERG

Jill Goldberg is drawn to simple, luxurious, and clean spaces. "Not a lot of froufrou: also not stark modern, but modern with a California slant," says Goldberg, whose design firm, Hudson Interior Designs, is located in Boston's South End. "It's nice to keep a traditional exterior. I love a classic shingled house where homeowners are willing to take more of a chance on the interior."

The seasoned designer has been impacted by interiors since she was a little girl—she vividly remembers the home of a family friend that deeply resonated with her. "I still remember everything about that magical space . . . an exploding mixture of textures and color. All of it tapped into something bold, abundant, upbeat, and unexpected," recalls Goldberg. An ever-changing selection of the designer's vision is on display at the home accessories trove she operates near her studio, also called Hudson.

As the internet and media outlets have opened up the endless possibilities of interior design to the public, Goldberg's clients have come to her armed with Pinterest boards and magazine cutouts depicting a range of décor inspirations. "In some cases, their eyes are bigger than their stomachs. They aren't quite ready to push the envelope as much in their own home, but the region is still evolving," says Goldberg, adding that one thing is for sure: people aren't trying to emulate the scheme they've seen at their neighbor's house. "They want their house to feel distinct and connected to who they are."

UPDATED ORIGINAL

Goldberg came on board at the very beginning for the renovation of this early 1900s Arts and Crafts–style home in the suburbs. The goal of the project was to give nods to the home's origins while lightening and modernizing the interior. In the dining room, tall wood wall paneling evokes the vertical-style wainscoting that was common in homes of the era, and a William Morris antique–inspired wall covering featuring a natural floral motif also contributes to the original nature of the home. While narrow plank oak floors are original to the home, the prominent Oly Studio chandelier, featuring a large grouping of glass bubbles, adds significant contemporary flair.

In the adjacent front hallway, an oversize spherical light fixture is a modern representation of a traditional style. Goldberg sheathed the ceiling with white textured wallpaper in a swirling motif. "The hallway is large, and we wanted to give the big expanse of ceiling some interest. It's a design element that looks like it could be an original detail," says Goldberg.

A time-honored appeal is achieved in the kitchen, where finely crafted custom white cabinetry is fitted with iron-period hardware. One bank of cabinetry features refined iron detailing and historic bubble glass fronts, another nod to the home's architectural origins. Yet the space is clearly suited for a modern family, with a sizeable banquette nestled up to a table in the eating area geared toward casual meals. Above the table, a chandelier made of glass globes that encase Edison bulbs adds subtle interest. "We didn't want a singular fixture that would feel heavy over the table, nor did we want two pendants," says Goldberg. "This one is clear and light, with the individual fixtures at different heights. You can see through it; it's not a big block of space."

The color palette throughout the home is neutral, allowing for the light and white painted woodwork to take center stage. The combination also helps integrate the original and new elements of the house, including a family room with a vaulted wood-clad ceiling, abundant windows, and a generous fireplace. "It's tough to tell what is new to the house and what was original," says Goldberg. "It's now an open, bright home that works for the way we live in the twenty-first century."

The sunroom features wood paneling in the style of many Arts and Crafts–era homes, while plush furniture ensures modern-day comfort.

LEFT: The new family room ceiling is lofted and clad with wood paneling; abundant long windows ensure the room is constantly filled with light. **ABOVE:** The original wood floors remain intact throughout most of the home.

CLOCKWISE, FROM THIS PAGE: The butler's pantry features a small sink integrated into the marble counter. A built-in banquette area at the kitchen table features small shelves and cabinets for storage. Rustic wicker Serena & Lily pendants hang above the kitchen island.

CLOCKWISE, FROM OPPOSITE PAGE: The top-floor bathroom features cement tile in a more traditional pattern. The master bathroom vanity has a timeless appeal. Smaller in size, the master bedroom's slight black pedestal tables were a perfect fit. The attic was converted into an arts and crafts room for the family.

AIRY INFLUENCE

In this classic gambrel-roofed Shingle-style home, the homeowner was willing to have "fun," says Goldberg. "She wanted to make it feel like a house in California that was bright and airy, while still retaining a New England sensibility." A built-in bar takes up one end of the den, where walls are painted a custom blend of blue and gray, creating an enveloping feel. Architectural details abound: Ceilings are coffered and walls have regal paneling that lends an air of formality. Vibrant patterned Roman shades have hints of green, coral, and blue.

Brass accents are used throughout the home, and rich moldings add character and depth to spaces. The first floor hallway has an arched ceiling and a herringbone-patterned wood floor. "It's the grandest part of the house," says Goldberg. The living room feels refined yet informal, a space where the key goal was for it to be a place where the family could relax and be comfortable. The ceiling is clad with shiplap paneling as a nod to a storied New England architectural element. While the color scheme is sedate here, the room is multidimensional, with an Imperial Danby marble on the fireplace surround, Stark's contemporary-yet-classic antelope-patterned carpet, and a piece of abstract art that Goldberg created.

To add interest to the white kitchen, a custom stainless steel and brass range hood was installed as a focal point. On the other side of the room, a two-tiered brass chandelier drops dramatically from the lofty ceiling. The modern stools are eye catching for their minimal form. "I didn't want anything with backs. There is a lot of traditional going on with the molding and cabinetry in here, so I wanted the stools to be modern and sort of fade away," says Goldberg.

Painted a deep, dark gray, the office is located on the opposite side of the house from the den. Here, Goldberg wanted to stabilize the heft of the den's rich blue-gray coloring with the heft of another richly-colored room. "The rug's geometric pattern paired with the brass-framed painting of a tortoise infuses the space with a bit of whimsy. "There are grass-woven shades on the windows," adds Goldberg. "A simple, chic take on the California vibe, which asserts the idea that no space in the house should feel too serious."

With the study's dark gray walls and a more masculine geometric print rug, the painting of the tortoise shell adds a bit of whimsy.

The Beacon Hill fabric on the den's Roman shades adds bursts of vibrant green and pink, colors reflected in more sedate tones throughout the room.

ABOVE: Brass was used throughout the home to infuse richness and a bit of glam. The hallway wood floor is laid in a herringbone pattern. **RIGHT:** Goldberg painted the piece above the mantle as a gift for the homeowners.

ABOVE: While most of the fixtures in the home are brass, nickel hardware on the cabinets adds a pleasing contrast and picks up the stainless steel of the hood. **OPPOSITE:** In many rooms, the windows are left unadorned to accent the rich moldings.

CLOCKWISE, FROM THIS PAGE: A vivid green four-poster bed from Room & Board is the highlight of one daughter's bedroom. The first-floor powder room features tropical-feeling Schumacher wallpaper, a tiny Restoration Hardware sink, and an Oly Studio mirror. In the other daughter's room, Goldberg called for the walls to be painted with alternating pink and white stripes. The New Ravenna herringbone tile on the master bathroom floor is a showpiece.

JILL LITNER KAPLAN

With a background in fashion merchandising and luxury goods in New York City and an MBA from Harvard Business School, Jill Litner Kaplan took a circuitous route to becoming an interior designer. Her multifaceted career path, paired with her passion for fashion, fine fabrics, and art, has served her well, enhancing her ability to create visually stimulating environments for her clients.

When Kaplan started her Newton, Massachusetts, firm fifteen years ago, the buzzwords for interior design may have well been "conservative, safe, and nothing risky," she says. "New Englanders were adorning their homes with oriental rugs and paintings of ships. The only colors people would use were red, blue, green, and mustard yellow," recalls Kaplan, who grew up in nearby Belmont.

A city long steeped in academic tradition, Boston, in recent years, has transitioned into a hub for high-tech industry. "That evolution has led to a considerable shift in interior design. There is a demographic of young people here who are taking risks professionally, and they are much more interested in taking design risks than the previous generation," says Kaplan, while noting that it's no longer just women who are involved in making the interior design decisions for their homes. "We frequently work with both members of a couple now. Often, they are each ambitious and outstanding in their careers. They have robust experiences that influence their design decisions."

Kaplan says that her New England childhood looks dramatically different than her own kids' childhoods. And that's a pretty universal theme. "There is a conscious decision throughout the region to leave behind the design environment of the past," says Kaplan. "People are making an effort to not live in a home like the one they grew up in. And the results are amazing."

REFINED ECLECTICISM

On her frequent travels across the country and abroad, Kaplan is always on the hunt for compelling art and wares for her clients. "I have a passion for finding extraordinary, unusual things," she says.

This suburban 1930s center-entrance Colonial contains a vibrant display of treasures collected by Kaplan. In the living room, a bold geometric painting by Alexander Calder, which she discovered on a jaunt to Los Angeles, hangs near an antique walnut coffee table with silver leaf procured at an estate sale. On top of the coffee table, antique silver tribal necklaces are displayed on stands. When Kaplan came on board, it was immediately apparent that the house had good bones and some revered architectural details, including pristine dentil moldings, yet the décor desperately needed some spark. "The wife has an unabashed love of color and she gave me free rein," says Kaplan, who strove to merge the older nature of the home with a new, modern feeling by "layering fabrics with beautiful found objects, lighting, and art."

Kaplan favors using neutral hues on walls—taupe and sandy grays—believing that color is best incorporated into rooms through art and textiles. She shifted from this position in the dining room, where the walls are painted a creamy blue. "I selected the color so that when you enter the house, the blues scattered throughout the living room mirror the color of the dining room, visually connecting them to one another," says Kaplan. "The furniture and rug in the dining room are quite neutral, and the blues are articulated in the pattern of the drapery and echoed in the artwork throughout."

Kaplan designed built-ins throughout the house for storage and to define spaces. To separate the family room from the foyer and living room, a wall of cabinetry is also a focal point, as it displays a lively mixed-media painting by artist Sally Egbert along with pieces of petrified wood and conch shells that sit on the open shelves. "Each one looks like a natural sculpture," says Kaplan.

The foyer is a compact space. "No matter what size the area is, the front entrance sets the stage for everything that follows in the first two seconds of walking into the home," says Kaplan, a notion she recalls from her days in merchandising. When she found a mother-of-pearl and bone-inlay cabinet, she knew at once it had the impact she was looking for. "It grabs the attention of guests walking through the door and signals that the rest of the home is special."

Kaplan unearthed the silver leaf and walnut coffee table in the living room at a local estate sale.

LEFT: A blue sofa from the family's former South End home was the only existing piece of furniture they wanted to incorporate in the living room. The triptych is by Boston artist John Thompson. **ABOVE:** Lamps from Boston Consignment incorporate the sofa's cobalt blue.

CLOCKWISE, FROM THIS PAGE:
Kaplan designed the family room built-in as a separation between the family room, the foyer, and the living room. An Italian Murano glass Sputnik chandelier hangs above the dining room table. Chairs in the family room feature a star outline in red.

CLOCKWISE, FROM THIS PAGE: Serene and multilayered, the master bedroom has an understated color palette. The live floral arrangements in the family room mimic the motif of a painting hung on the wall. In one daughter's bedroom, Kaplan hung Chinese knife paintings that feel youthful. For another daughter's bedroom, shades of blue are paired with white and accented by colorful prints.

COLOR STORY

This family residence is the antithesis of going for a more calming palette, says Kaplan. "The home has a tremendous amount of color, texture, and rich pattern." Early on, the homeowners expressed that they wanted the home to feel warm and enveloping, a mood that was achieved in the living room with layers of distinctive textiles and textural elements. The room scheme originated with drapes made from a Martyn Lawrence Bullard fabric in a lively Suzani motif that create an appealing juxtaposition with a pair of sofas upholstered in custom tweed, a coffee table made of bone, and a Mongolian lamb-upholstered bench. "The furniture in here is quite close, so it creates a very intimate setting. All of these interesting textures tell their own stories," says Kaplan.

In the adjacent dining room, the same Suzani drapes create cohesion, and a vintage-inspired Sputnik chandelier draws the eye upward. The fixture is brass, as are the sconces and drapery rods, a material selected for its ability to infuse warmth and richness.

A key part of the project involved creating spaces for the family of five to be together. An expansive lower-level family room incorporates multiple areas to lounge along with a game table where the group gathers for Monopoly. "The homeowner was really fearless when it came to color," says Kaplan. "We went a little wild in here with plums and aubergines,

the pinks and purples, and the pairing of patterns: stripes, plaids, and polka dots. But it works. The room, along with the adjacent arts and crafts room—fitted with fun Kartell pink Lucite light pendants—is a true magnet for the family's three teenage girls.

Kaplan has a voracious appetite for art. "It doesn't matter what room in the house it is, from the public spaces to kids' rooms, every room deserves great art," she says. In one of the daughter's rooms, a quartet of vivid botanical paintings by artist Laura Kramer emanates a cheerful glow in one corner.

At the end of the hall, Kaplan created a seating area in the landing for the girls to congregate in front of the bay window. A light fixture is made of mother-of-pearl shell material fashioned into butterflies, which is symbolic of the mood evoked throughout the residence, says Kaplan. "The home is unabashedly feminine and sweet; it has an exuberance and lightness of being. Everywhere you turn, there is this sense of happiness."

OPPOSITE: In the lower-level media room, Kaplan created multiple areas for the family to congregate.
ABOVE: For each of the children's rooms, Kaplan designed desks with plenty of storage.

CLOCKWISE, FROM OPPOSITE PAGE: Shades of yellow, the wife's favorite color, are woven throughout the living and dining area. Drapes with a Suzani pattern draw the eye toward the window. A multihued print hangs above a bone inlay chest in the bedroom.

ABOVE: A craft room on the lower level features pleasing pops of pink, including rose-tinted Kartell light fixtures. **OPPOSITE:** Kaplan created a cozy nook with chairs on the second-floor landing.

CLOCKWISE, FROM THIS PAGE:
In one of the daughter's rooms, paintings by Laura Kramer are hung above chairs upholstered in a magenta-toned Harlequin fabric. Shades of plum, pink, and purple give the media room a playful vibe, while sophisticated patterns and artwork keep the room from feeling too youthful. Though the foyer is small, Kaplan insisted the space be a standout.

ANA DONOHUE

When it comes to Ana Donohue's personal aesthetic, she loves anything unexpected and slightly imperfect. She has a fondness for traditional Italian-inspired pieces "with ornate cures in wood and iron that have a masculine feel," says Donohue, who spent several years working as an international flight attendant prior to becoming a designer. "During that period, in my twenties, I had the opportunity to see architecture and design all over the world and that had a big influence on me, ultimately leading me to pursue a design career," she says, adding that another one of her favorite decorative elements is "1970s art combined with contemporary pieces here and there to calm things down."

The pairing of styles and eras is a cornerstone of Donohue's Melrose, Massachusetts, firm, though she realizes that not everyone wants to go quite to the level of her personal taste. Her main objective is to create rooms with vibrancy. "I push my clients a little sometimes," says Donohue. "I want to get them out of their comfort zones and play a bit." Such a feat has become easier than it was when she first started her interior design career in 2002.

"Back then, clients wanted very much what was expected—no one would go too far out of the box," recalls Donohue. "People are now much more focused on creating an individual design that works specifically for them. They're more confident in their choices, more willing to go in different directions with material selections. They aren't shying away when we suggest mixing furniture and being edgier."

RESIDENTIAL REBOOT

Donohue gets more creative license these days when she designs a second or third home for a client. "At that point, they really trust me; they let me play more and aren't worried when I suggest something unexpected." Such was the case for this suburban Cape Cod–style house she recently redesigned; she had designed a smaller residence for the homeowners before they had kids. "This is to be their forever home," says Donohue, who conceived a top-to-bottom overhaul for the expansive residence.

Donohue was tasked with making the dated, devoid-of-character house family friendly while also creating a sophisticated presence. Timeless architectural details including coffered ceilings and wainscoting—which reveals hidden storage compartments in some spots—were added to the living and dining rooms. In the kitchen, which overlooks a vast spread of conservation land, Donohue designed a wall of iron-trimmed windows and doors. "It brings in so much light, which really filters from here throughout the whole house," she says. While the homeowners initially considered a white-and-gray kitchen, Donohue eschewed the combination as too trendy and steered them toward lighter gray cabinetry that has brown tinting paired with red-toned wood. "You see so many trees through the kitchen windows and the reddish wood of the cabinetry evokes the trees, bringing some of what you're seeing out there inside."

Color, one of Donohue's favorite elements, figured largely into the new scheme. "We wanted to make the rooms exuberant and inviting," she says. The jumping-off point for a bright, lively aesthetic was the multihued velvet S. Harris fabric the designer selected for the high-backed barrel chairs in the living room. "I don't start with rugs; I tend to kick off the design with a really great fabric," says Donohue, who picked up tones of fuchsia and green from the fabric for the velvet upholstery on the dining room chairs. A flash of turquoise depicted in the fabric matches the color of a Roche Bobois console table in the room. The colors repeat throughout the home—turquoise was used on the vanity in a bathroom where walls are sheathed in lavender grass cloth, another hue found in that S. Harris fabric.

A similar shade of lavender is found in the family room rug while the rest of the room is a play on black and white, per the homeowners' wishes. Donohue managed to make the more sedate hues feel modern and layered by pairing them with a hand-painted fireplace surround, a chaise upholstered in a Fabricut pattern, and a wall installation that depicts twigs fashioned out of metal, another nod to the home's tree-shrouded landscape.

Just inside the front door, an animal hide rug is among the first elements one sees when entering the home.

ABOVE: The open living and dining areas make it possible for multiple people to be comfortable during large gatherings. **OPPOSITE:** The dining room's Roche Bobois furniture has a formal appeal without feeling too fussy.

CLOCKWISE, FROM THIS PAGE: At one end of the kitchen, a bar area separates the space from the family room. Lucite counter stools are both modern and family friendly. A mirrored chandelier bounces light around the space. The mix of light gray and wood cabinetry in the kitchen exudes warmth.

OPPOSITE: An array of textures makes the family room's black-and-white palette feel diverse and multifaceted. **ABOVE:** Located off of the garage, the mudroom has ample storage and an intriguing aesthetic.

CLEAN LIVING

The Newbury Street location of this residence was exactly what the homeowners had in mind during their search for a pied-à-terre. With windows that stretch from the floor nearly all the way to the ceiling in the main living space, the view of the bustling city makes for a wonderful backdrop. "We simplified everything in the room so the space could be all about the views," says Donohue, adding that another reason she strove for a clean, modern interior vibe was because the exterior façade of the building—a former school—is very traditional.

A deep midnight blue was used for the wall color, while the trim around the windows is painted a crisp white. Slim privacy shades are the window's sole adornment. "I'm normally a big window-treatment person, but we didn't want anything to impact the view," says Donohue. To enhance the airy appeal, the dark walnut floors were stripped and bleached to a much lighter hue. Furnishings, including a low-backed neutral sofa and linear navy leather chairs, are spare and streamlined.

Infusions of color are minimal and strategic, throw pillows add a little pizazz, and art gives distinct energy to certain areas. Three small abstract paintings atop a bank of shelves feature vivid orange tones that work in cohesion with the citrus-hued glass light fixture above the dining table.

In the master bedroom, both the walls and the trim are painted white. Donohue accented the clean palette with notes of texture and color in the bedding. "The thing with going for a contemporary look is that you have to make sure it doesn't feel too cold," she says. "Art, textiles, and wood can be incorporated to add warmth." In the daughters' bedroom, where walls are also white, a more youthful vibe is achieved with bold pops of color, including a whimsical orange area rug fashioned after a mod animal hide.

Donohue devised a modern take on the traditional bookshelf near the dining table.

ABOVE: By leaving the windows unadorned, the home is privy to optimal views of the city. **OPPOSITE:** The dark walnut floors were stained and bleached to lighten up the space. A Jonathan Adler desk adds warmth to the room.

The key with white walls and spare furniture, says Donohue, is to not let the space feel too cold. Here, warmth was introduced with textiles and art.

LEFT: The girls' room, with layers of pink and yellow, is vibrant and fun. **ABOVE:** The Ann Sacks tile on the shower walls infuses color into the streamlined bathroom.

RESOURCES

LIZ CAAN
LIZ CAAN & CO.
1064 & 1066 Centre Street
Newton, MA 02549
617-244-0424; lizcaan.com

PAULA DAHER
DAHER INTERIOR DESIGN
224 Clarendon Street
Boston, MA 02116
617-236-0355; daherinteriordesign.com

ANA DONOHUE
ANA DONOHUE INTERIORS
31 Harvard Street
Melrose, MA 02176
617-331-2663; anadonohueinteriors.com

DEE ELMS
ELMS INTERIOR DESIGN
535 Albany Street, 4th Floor
Boston, MA 02118
617-451-1555; elmsid.com

TOM EGAN & JOSH LINDER
EVOLVE RESIDENTIAL
89 West Concord Street
Boston, MA 02118
617-424-0003; evolveresidential.com

ROBIN GANNON
ROBIN GANNON INTERIORS & HOME
1656 Massachusetts Avenue
Lexington, MA 02420
781-862-0466; robingannoninteriors.com

ELIZABETH GEORGANTAS
GEORGANTAS DESIGN + DEVELOPMENT
Boston, MA 02108
617-941-4800; livegeorgantas.com

JILL GOLDBERG
HUDSON INTERIOR DESIGNS
12 Union Park Street
Boston, MA 0118
617-292-0900; hudsoninteriordesigns.com

JILL LITNER KAPLAN
JILL LITNER KAPLAN INTERIORS
West Newton, MA 02465
617-558-7751; jilllitnerkaplan.com

RACHEL REIDER
RACHEL REIDER INTERIORS
535 Albany Street, 2nd Floor
Boston, MA 02118
617-942-2460; rachelreider.com

OPPOSITE: Spiral staircase design by Paula Daher.

PAGE 200: Living room design by Robin Gannon.

ACKNOWLEDGMENTS

New England Modern came to fruition thanks to the efforts of numerous supportive people. I am grateful to my editor, Katie Killebrew, for embracing the book concept from the get-go. You believed in my ability to produce this manuscript without very much to go on. You asked for a few details and then said, "Go for it." I know from experience that this is not typically how book deals come together.

Photographer Michael J. Lee, my longtime collaborator and friend, thank you for jumping on board immediately. I could never, in a million years, have taken on this project without you. Your stunning photography gave this book life.

My deepest heartfelt gratitude goes to Ana, Dee, Elizabeth, Jill G., Jill K., Josh, Liz, Paula, Rachel, Robin, and Tom. You designers are the best, your talent is immeasurable—your work speaks volumes. Thank you for supporting me and for being involved in this project. I am so glad to know you all.

I'm grateful to my parents, who gave me the foundation upon which I've based my career. While none of us knew it at the time, all those antiquing excursions and renovation projects influenced me indelibly.

Most of all, I thank my husband, Michael Hogan, for always encouraging me to say "yes" even when the process seems daunting—for cheering me on and keeping me focused. With you in my corner, all things seem possible.

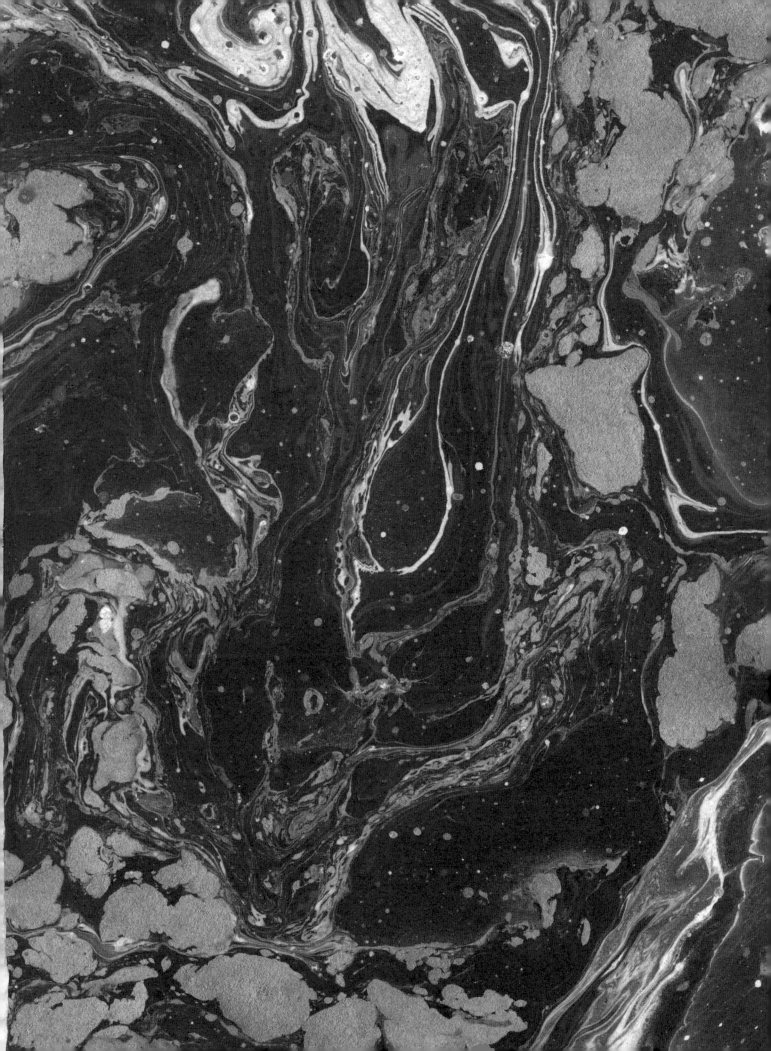

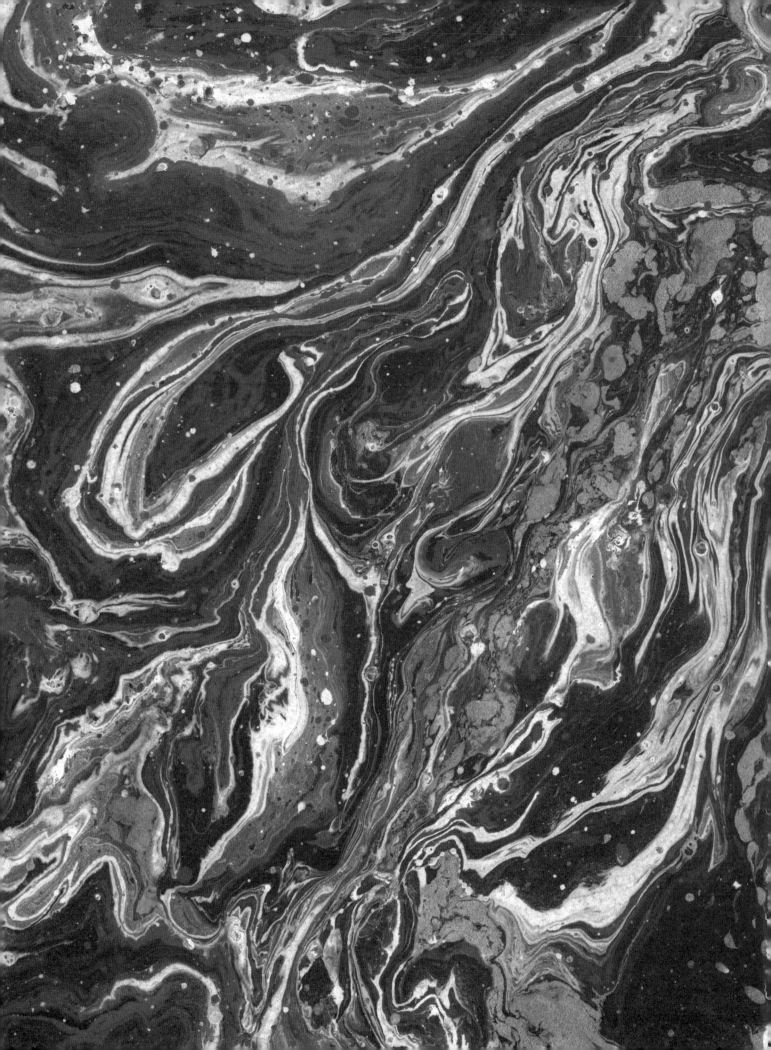